Organizational Goal Structures

The West Series in Business Policy and Planning

Strategy Formulation: Analytical Concepts
Charles W. Hofer and Dan Schendel

Strategy Implementation: The Role of Structure and Process
Jay R. Galbraith and Daniel A. Nathanson

Organizational Goal Structures
Max D. Richards

Strategy Formulation: Political Concepts
Ian C. MacMillan

Organizational Goal Structures

Max D. Richards
The Pennsylvania State University

West Publishing Company
St. Paul   New York   Los Angeles   San Francisco

COPYRIGHT © 1978 By WEST PUBLISHING CO.
50 West Kellogg Boulevard
P.O. Box 3526
St. Paul, Minnesota 55165

Printed in the United States of America

Library of Congress Cataloging in Publication Data

Richards, Max De Voe, 1923—
    Organizational goal structures.

    (The West series in business policy and planning)
    Bibliography: p.

    Includes index.

    1. Industrial management. 2. Corporate planning.
I. Title.
HD38.R472   658.4'02   78–1867
ISBN 0–8299–0210–4

Contents

Foreword

The purpose of this common foreword to all the volumes in the *West Series on Business Policy and Planning* is threefold: first, to provide background to the reader on the origins and purposes of the series; second, to describe the overall design of the series and the contents of the texts contained in the series; and third, to describe ways in which the series or the individual texts within it can be used.

This series is a response to the rapid and significant changes that have occurred in the policy area over the past fifteen years. While business policy is a subject of long standing in management schools, it has traditionally been viewed as a capstone course whose primary purpose was to *integrate* the knowledge and skills students had gained in the functional disciplines. During the past decade, however, policy has developed a substantive content of its own that has permitted it to emerge as a discipline in its own right. Originally, this content focused on the concept of organizational strategy and on the processes by which such strategies were formulated and implemented within organizations. More recently, the scope of the field has broadened to include the study of all the functions and responsibilities of top management, together with the organizational processes and systems for formulating and implementing organizational strategy. To date, however, this extension in scope has not been reflected in texts in the field.

The basic purpose of the *West Series on Business Policy and Planning* is to fill this void through the development of a series of texts that cover the policy field while incorporating the latest research findings and conceptual thought.

In designing the series, we took care to ensure, not only that the various texts fit together as a series, but also that each text is self-contained and addresses a major topic in the field.   In addition, each text is written so that it can be used at both the advanced undergraduate and the masters level.   The first four texts, which cover topics in the heart of the policy field, are:

Organizational Goal Structures, by Max D. Richards.

Strategy Formulation: Analytical Concepts, by Charles W. Hofer and Dan Schendel.

Strategy Formulation: Political Concepts, by Ian C. MacMillan.

Strategy Implementation: The Role of Structure and Process, by Jay R. Galbraith and Daniel A. Nathanson.

A second set of texts are in preparation and should be available next year.   They will cover additional topics in policy and planning such as the behavioral and social systems aspects of the strategy formulation process, environment forecasting, strategic control, formal planning systems, and the strategic management of new ventures. Additional texts covering still other topics are being considered for the years following.

The entire series has been designed so that the texts within it can be used in several ways.   First, the individual texts can be used to supplement the conceptual materials contained in existing texts and case books in the field.   In this regard, explicit definitions are given for those terms and concepts for which there is as yet no common usage in the field, and, whenever feasible, the differences between these definitions and those in the major texts and case books are noted.   Second, one or more of the series texts can be combined with cases drawn from the Intercollegiate Case Clearing House to create a hand-crafted case course suited to local needs.   To assist those interested in such usage, most texts in the series include a list of ICCH cases that could be used in conjunction with it.   Finally, the series can be used without other materials by those who wish to teach a theory-oriented policy course.   Thus, the series offers the individual instructor flexibility in designing a policy course.   Finally, because of their self-contained nature, each of the texts can also be used as a supplement to various nonpolicy courses within business and management school curricula.

Charles W. Hofer

Dan Schendel

Consulting Editors

September, 1977

Preface

This book is an introduction to the study of organizational goals and goal processes. As such, it is written for the attention of managers, planners, and students of organizational strategy and policy who wrestle with the questions of what purposes their activities should serve. The book is presented with the practitioner in mind, rather than the acamedic researcher or scholar. Thus, references are sacrificed for more examples that clarify the concepts and behaviors shown.

There are several different streams of thought about goals. These conceptual approaches have lacked an integrated treatment in the past:

1) the economic and management science literature, focusing upon optimization of a narrowly conceived set of goals;

2) the behavioral and political science literature, which criticizes the reality of the classical economic approaches;

3) the strategy-policy-planning literature, which is concerned with establishing and implementing an overall framework for organizational functioning;

4) the social responsibility literature that to some extent is exhortive, yet relevant, to establishing goals or constraints to be dealt with; and

5) the Management by Objectives (MBO) literature, the major concerns of which involve establishing and reviewing performance against specific goals of a subordinate with his superior.

Although these topical areas and concepts are presented, the purpose is to integrate these materials in such a way that the manager can

—establish goals of his organization consistent in an economic, social, technological, and political manner with its environments. This problem involves not only the question of whether the organization is to be viable, but also whether it is considered legitimate in the eyes of larger society.

—formulate and achieve goals and patterns of goals that are realistic in terms of achievement. Restructuring internal operations or establishing goals consistent with internal operations are problems central to this task.

The reader should recognize that although overall goals reflect the final purposes toward which an organization strives, the means for achieving objectives through plans, strategies, and political processes cannot be treated in depth in this book. Three companion books in the West Series on Business Policy and Planning treat these topics extensively. Charles Hofer and Dan Schendel examine *Strategy Formulation: Analytical Concepts*. They provide the approaches used to achieve top-level goals and the sources of goals sought at lower levels. Ian MacMillan in his *Strategy Formulation: Political Concepts* shows how goals and organizational intentions are formed and sometimes distorted by individuals and subgroups in a system. Jay Galbraith and Daniel Nathanson in their *Strategy Implementation: The Role of Structure and Process* examine environmental conditions and internal processes that influence goal achievement. Together these four books form an integrated package for the study of organizational strategy.

At the same time, organizational goals cannot be discussed without reference to strategy formulation and implementation. As a consequence, this book, although focusing upon goals and goal processes, integrates formulation and implementation of strategy.

The order of the chapters reflect the several literature streams noted above. Chapters one and two focus on the nature of goals and goal patterns. Chapter three examines coalitions, power, goal formation processes, and patterns of goals resulting therefrom. Chapter four examines social issues and values as they impinge upon, or are embraced by, the functioning in an organization. Chapter five relates those aspects of formal planning systems that have particular implications to organizational objectives. Chapter six is devoted to the MBO process. Finally, chapter seven is an integration of these concepts with a view to providing the manager with approaches he can in fact employ to merge the materials in this book into his day-to-day activities.

Both the creation of new knowledge and the combining of existing knowledge into new forms for new insights and perspectives are important tasks. Although this book does not present new research findings, it does attempt to integrate materials on goals in new ways to provide the manager and the student of management policy perspective and approaches for better management by the use of goals.

This book could never have been completed in the planned time frame without the cooperation and dedication of three other people. Dr. Robert Pashek was kind enough to go on vacation at just the right time so that his secretary, Ruth Nixon, could draft and redraft the manuscript. Ruth was particularly helpful and kind in her efforts, in spite of the fact that she might have "enjoyed" the vacation of her boss. Dan Schendel was most insightful and insistent about integrating the material to the *West Series on Business Policy and Planning*.

I am indebted to all but responsible alone.

Max Richards
September, 1977
University Park, PA

†

1

The Nature of
Goals in Organizations

"We are seeking a 15 percent return on invested capital after taxes and a 10 percent growth in sales per year," states the chief executive officer of a large building products enterprise. He continues, "These overall corporate goals were established by our chairman to motivate company personnel to be number one in our industry and to be able to attract capital from the investment community in competition with leaders in other industries. After all, in the capital markets we compete with all companies; in our industry we compete with a relatively small group of firms." This statement infers that return on invested capital, growth, and a leading industry position are desirable for the firm to achieve, in light of what other firms within and outside the industry are achieving. The chairman of the board of directors is externally oriented in his views toward establishing corporate objectives, as he relies on the capital and competitive markets to influence his thinking about what his organization ought to achieve.

In discussing how these overall corporate objectives influence operations within the company, two major kinds of thinking emerge: one is strategic in character, affecting the nature of the businesses in which the firm engages; the second is operational in nature in that it influences how lower-level managers formulate these overall corporate goals into objectives for their own parts of the corporation.

As to the strategic influence of these overall goals, the chief executive continues, "As you know, we have a substantial sales volume in packaging. Our competitors appear to be satisfied with a 6 percent return on investment so that premium pricing to attain our investment goal is limited, in spite of the considerable research and development we undertake to provide our packaging with a superior capability. Even with our efforts, we are unable to come close to our overall goal. The low returns on packaging products lower our overall returns on capital and need to be offset by substantially higher profits from other product lines. We would sell this business in packaging quickly if we could obtain Federal Trade Commission approval." This statement illustrates several other dimensions in the use of goals:

1. A business with low returns becomes a candidate for divestiture. Conversely, businesses with high returns are presumably encouraged. The goals influence the strategy of the firm by the businesses that are discouraged or encouraged.

2. The internal management and allocation of resources is directly influenced, in this instance, within the packaging part of the business. Research and development is high to provide superior product characteristics and a higher price, supposedly to attain higher-than-competitive margins and returns. As competitors focus on "commodity" product designs sold primarily on the basis of price, this firm counters by achieving a differentiated product design sold at higher prices.

3. A third implication of the above statement is the reference to constraint by the government (F.T.C.) in divesting the packaging line. The strategic choice is not free from government influence. Goal setting and achievement is constrained by external factors in the environment other than competitors and customers.

In commenting on how the overall corporate goals influence lower-level managers, the president stated: "Although many managers cannot relate their operations directly to return on investment, they have developed their own goals and guidelines to mesh their subactivities with overall corporate objectives. Our advertising director, for example, allocates advertising dollars for a new product to gain rapid customer acceptance and market share before competitors can copy it and drive down the price. Conversely, our production managers cannot pay attention only to minimizing the costs of production. They must remain flexible to introduce new production processes and materials required by the continuous stream of new designs." This statement provides us with examples of how individual submanagers are influenced by the overall corporate-level goals to establish their own goals and guides to decisions.

The relevance of this somewhat extended example of goal establishment and managerial behavior is that:

1. Establishing corporate-level goals can provide useful guidelines to both strategic and operating decisions.

2. Internal systems are designed to accomplish higher-level objectives *if* there is acceptance of the legitimacy of overall goals.

3. All organizations have goals reflecting the achievement of some purpose. These goals can either be explicit, as in the above example, or they can be implicit and poorly stated, as other subsequent examples will amplify.

4. There is a structure of goals in an organization. Some goals stem from higher-level goals. The goal of production flexibility stems from the goals of high margins and product innovation. These, in turn, are designed to serve the overall profitability goal. In addition to such a vertical consistency in goals, those at any one level of organization ought to be consistent with each other. This matrix of goals could be thought of so that each item in a horizontal row of the matrix represents results to be achieved at a single level of organization. Ideally, each goal in the row would be consistent with every other in the same row. In addition, each expected result would be designed to contribute to the achievement of the goals of the next higher row in the matrix. As will be shown, not all (or sometimes none) of these results occur in an organization. If organizations have unclear and conflicting goals, subordinate behaviors can vary widely, because each individual perceives a different set of ends to be achieved. Thus, the building products company is an example of a system that has utilized goals and goal processes in an explicit, coordinated manner to reach specific and difficult goals.

THE PURPOSE OF THIS BOOK

Society is concerned about the leadership and effective administration of its institutions, because the values resulting from an organization's operations are recognized as being influenced by the quality of its managerial efforts. The managers of organizations express a similar concern, reflected by the continual development of a host of techniques and approaches to better management. Short courses and educational development programs to upgrade managerial knowledge and skills abound. Some developments are fads that soon fade from the scene. Others are of more lasting value and become either part of the agenda of basic management knowledge or an item in the "approved" repertoire of managerial skills.

Organizational goals and the processes of establishing them are not fads. They are basic features of all organized group activity. The perceptions that an enterprise's participants have of its objectives are critical to whether they join and remain effective contributors in creating the values society expects from the institution they serve.

ORGANIZATION OF THE BOOK

In spite of the centrality of goals to organizational performance, few, if any, integrations of the existing knowledge about the relevance, establishment, and use of organizational goals exist. It is the central purpose of this text to provide a comprehensive overview of goals and the processes useful to managers and students of management in establishing and using goals. To accomplish this purpose, this chapter undertakes an exposition on some basic concepts about goals; organizations and their goals are more specific, however, so patterns of goals at different levels of organizations emerge. The second chapter is devoted to examining these patterns, particularly as they relate to the long-run top management decisions.

To provide an understanding of how goals emerge, become institutionalized, or fade away, the third chapter examines issues of power, the formation of group coalitions, and their processes in establishing goals and related topics. By understanding such essentially political processes, the manager can more relevantly direct his personal behavior, as he seeks to establish and employ goals in his managerial approaches.

Society is expressing concern over the operation of many of its institutions. Big government is called unresponsive, big unions irresponsible, hospitals expensive, universities inefficient, and business concerned only with profits. The questions examined in chapter four involve how organizations respond to external pressures, what changes in social values are impinging upon organizations, and whether the goals of institutions designed in the past are consistent with these changes. The issues examined focus more upon whether an organization is viable in society, rather than upon how to manage through goals.

Chapters five and six do concern issues, problems, and approaches to managing with goals as a central focus. Long-range planning is an accepted activity that uses and affects the formal goals of a system.   Understanding these interrelations provides perspective for both processes.   Managing by objectives (MBO) has become a catchword for a process through which a manager and his subordinate focus on the important things to be accomplished, that is, the objectives that the subordinate should achieve together with a review of past achievements toward prior stated objectives.   The final chapter summarizes, integrates, and provides summary perspectives to goals and goal processes.

The orientation of this text is toward the policy and strategic choices made by managers.   It is an integral part of the *West Series on Policy and Planning* and is designed to relate to the other texts in the study of organizational strategy and policy.   At the same time, the relevance of goals to the whole managerial process (whether at top, intermediate, or lower management levels) allows this book to be used by itself.

GOAL DEFINITIONS

This book is concerned with an examination of goals and goal processes.   Some writers differentiate between goals and objectives, but although one author might define objectives as the means for achieving overall goals, another might reverse this definition.   In this book, *goals, objectives, purposes*, and *ends* are considered interchangeable. A goal is defined as a planned position or result to be achieved.

Objectives have both a content and a level component.   A business firm can have an objective of profitability, or it could alternatively select an objective of achieving the highest quality of products in its industry.   The differential content of these goals will, when followed rationally, result in different behaviors within the organization, since quality is not necessarily consistent with profitability.

Either explicitly or implicitly, each goal also has a level component. If the content of the goal is profitability as measured by the return on equity, establishing a return on equity goal of "that consistent with the industry" implies an average return on equity for the firm. This level is, obviously, different from an alternative level that could be stated "to achieve the highest return on equity of any firm in our industry."   Both the content of the goal and its level influence behaviors within the organization and, therefore, require careful consideration in their establishment.

OPEN VERSUS CLOSED GOALS

Goals may be stated in general terms such as "to achieve better health." This is an open-ended goal, since it is never completely achieved; one presumably could always have better health. A closed goal is achievable and "closed" when met. "To reduce my heartbeat at rest to 55 per minute and my blood pressure to 120/80 in six months" is an example of a closed-end goal. Hofer and Schendel, in examining strategy formulation in this *West Series on Policy and Planning*, use "objective" to identify a closed-end goal. Thus, they differentiate between goals and objectives by denoting open-ended purposes as goals and closed-ended purposes as objectives. In this book, the context of the analysis is used to differentiate whether or not a goal is open or closed.

For realistic use by an organization, however, an open goal is valuable primarily as an intermediate step in establishing a closed-end objective. A higher quality product can be operationalized as a closed-end objective by greater specificity as to level and time frame involved. A mail-order book club sought to reduce errors. Both shipping the wrong book and billing incorrect amounts were identified as quality problems in their service. The objective established was "to decrease shipping and billing errors to 1 percent of orders within one year." To achieve this quality level, order filling and invoicing systems were reorganized, and increased management attention was given to the processes.

Results expected stated as open-ended goals do not allow management to know whether or not they have ever been achieved. Realistically, then, the management can use goals much more effectively and efficiently if they are stated in closed terms. Later in this chapter, we examine their specificity as a means to make goals more useful.

To arrive at a managerially useful closed-end goal, then, the following are needed:

content	high quality
a measure or indicator	errors made
a level	1 percent of orders
time period	one year

ENDS-MEANS-ENDS CHAINS

The aspirations of a professional football team may be to win the Super Bowl. To accomplish this, the coach may establish a strategy to emphasize his defensive platoon in the following season. In consultation with the defensive coordinator, he may then determine a goal to limit opponents to an average of 125 yards or less per game during the season. Note that the defensive goal was based upon the strategy of defensive emphasis. The strategy was selected as the best way to achieve a higher-level goal: winning the Super Bowl. Thus:

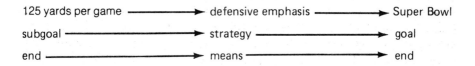

This example illustrates the differences between strategies and goals. A strategy is a set of actions, policies governing actions, and plans of activity to achieve given results; a goal is a result aspired to. But notice that a strategy provides also additional lower-level goals to be sought by subordinates in the organization, that is, the defensive coordinator.

The defensive coordinator may subsequently establish a defensive strategy (for example, minimal rushing of the opposing passer). Such a strategy will in turn be the basis for other subgoals of the defensive line, ends, linebackers, cornerbacks, and deep secondary unit. Each goal generates a strategy that in turn generates a further series of subgoals. This ends-means-ends process can be continued from the top to the bottom of an organization.

It should be noted that the defensive emphasis can only be rationally selected as the best means of achieving a Super Bowl win if the strength and weaknesses of opponents have been scouted to determine that a balanced offensive-defensive strategy or an offensive strategy would not be superior. Furthermore, complementary objectives for the offensive unit, too, need to be established in light of the defensive strategic orientation.

PURPOSES SERVED BY GOALS

An objective provides *guidance* to the direction of the efforts of individuals in a system. One toy manufacturer has high quality in terms of durability, usefulness, and function as one of its goals. Alternatively, a toy firm could have the objective of providing the cheapest, highest volume toys on the market. These two objectives would certainly lead the design and engineering of their toys toward different functional strategies. The effort required to achieve high quality and durability engenders high engineering and manufacturing costs not consistent with low price and highest volume of sales. A statement of either of these goals, however, would help guide the functional strategies in the design, engineering, manufacturing, and selling departments in consistent directions.

Similarly, goals affect the *planning* that the organization undertakes. A firm attempting to grow at a rapid rate and to increase its market share will require a planning effort that carefully examines the particular customers, their uses of the products involved, the potential for more sales to those customers, the same sort of analysis for unsold customers, the probable attractiveness of the firm's products to customers, etc. Efforts to achieve high levels of new product introduction would be probable. More extensive and intensive planning would be required in order to achieve the growth goal than if the objective were stability and maintenance of market share.

The use of objectives can provide *motivation* and inspiration to individuals in the organization to perform at higher levels of efficiency and effectiveness. Closed objectives establish the level of expectations for performance. Of course, individuals can establish their own goals and so be motivated by them. A student establishing and committing himself to an "A" average, for example, provides self-motivation and inspiration to his efforts. The manager, too, can establish personal goals. Yet, it is to the organizational goals that subordinate behavior must be directed and motivated. To ensure motivation, the manager needs to examine through ends-means-ends analysis the logic of what is expected for subordinates to achieve.

Objectives also form the basis for *evaluating* and *controlling* activity. The United Fund campaign in a moderate sized city might establish a goal of contributions from individuals as five dollars per capita. Such a goal would engender plans by the subchairman in charge of contacting individuals for solicitation, approaches to solicitation, and efforts of volunteers to obtain contributions and pledges. If, during the campaign, a contribution level of only four dollars per capita was being achieved, control efforts to determine why the variance occurred, whether it was due to the plans, the levels of the goal established in the first place, or other reasons could be examined for revision of subsequent behaviors.

Thus, goals and objectives permeate the whole management process, providing an underpinning for planning efforts, direction, motivation, and control. In organizations, managers are involved in these activities on a continual basis. Without goals and communication of them, behaviors in terms of managerial processes can meander in any direction. If you don't know where you are going, why start? Or if you start, what difference does it make in where your efforts are being applied? Or, if you don't know where you are going, any road will take you there.

ORGANIZATIONS AS GOAL SEEKING ENTITIES

Can an organization exist without having a goal? Is there such a thing as an organization that does not pursue at least a survival goal? In examining the behavior of some organizations, observers may find it difficult to identify the particular goal that is being pursued. In discussing goals, however, Krech and Crutchfield (1948, p. 370) state: "A group does not merely mean individuals characterized by some similar property. Thus, for example, a collection of Republicans or farmers, or Negroes or blind men is not a group." Gibb (1954, p. 879) states that a functional group "refers to two or more organisms interacting, in the pursuit of a common goal, in such a way that the existence of many is utilized for the satisfaction of some needs of each." Thus, in the view of Gibb, as well as Cyert and March (1963), Simon (1964) and others, an organization would not exist unless it undertook the satisfaction of some common objective. By definition, an organization has a goal or goals.

While organizations are goal seeking, the variation in forming and using objectives is wide. At one extreme are organizations that have established profitability as a single goal whose achievement is relentlessly and diligently pursued. At the opposite end of the spectrum stands an organization whose goals are not stated explicitly, whose statements are unclear to many members of the organization, and whose internal behaviors seem to range so widely that they could be interpreted as contributing to several disparate goals. In fact, it may appear that individuals are following lines of activity that maximize their personal values rather than those of the organization. Can such a minimally achieving organization compete and remain viable when opposed in the market by a goal oriented organization? It is to the explanation of how these differences can occur and their relevance to the manager in his use of objectives that the rest of this book is addressed. Both organizations have goals. One has a single objective, the other, many; one is a high achiever, the other, low.

They represent extremes between which the majority of organizations operate.

MULTIPLE GOALS

Peter Drucker (1954) was one of the early analysts to contend that organizations do and should undertake the achievement of multiple rather than single goals. Classical marginal productivity theory in economics assumes the singularity of profitability as the goal of the business firm in a competitive society. Drucker attacks the notion of emphasizing only profit when he contends that it misdirects managerial effort and encourages the worst practices of management. Specifically, short-run results are favored to the detriment of long-run viability and profitability. Postponable expenses and investments are avoided so that profits and returns during current periods are maximized while jeopardizing longer-term performance. Maintenance expenses can be reduced in a current period at the risk of serious breakdowns later. Research and development to replace maturing products can be delayed to show better current profits.

To balance long- and short-run considerations, Drucker suggests eight key areas in which overall corporate objectives of a business should be established: market standing; innovation; productivity; physical and financial resources; profitability; manager performance and development; worker performance and attitude; and public responsibility. If any of these areas are neglected, it results in subsequent unfavorable consequences. To illustrate, consider the need for objectives in managerial development. The experience of a medium-sized life insurance company is instructive in this instance. The company saw during the late 1950s and early 1960s market opportunities for new forms of life insurance and undertook an aggressive growth program. Since it had operated with a lean management structure, it had avoided management development that would have provided a cadre of qualified managers to meet the continuing and expanding need for managers in the company. As a result, the top management raided the ranks of competitors to obtain qualified managers to fill the new managerial positions opened up through anticipated growth. To attract managers from outside the firm, premium compensation packages had to be offered them. The lack of attention to management development goals consistent with other goals of the firm had these results:

1. Overhead costs exceeded competitors' because of the high compensation costs for the newly hired managers.

2. Morale of managers who had been with the firm declined because attractive openings were filled from the outside rather than from within. Further, the compensation given outsiders created pay inequities with older personnel.

3. While highly qualified individuals were attracted to the firm, the integration of their duties into those of others took several years of subpar performance as the system was being shaken down.

4. During the shakedown period of low performance, competitors made rapid strides in entrenching themselves in the markets originally attractive to the firm and the rationale for the growth it sought.

This example provides support to the Drucker thesis that lack of attention to one key area can have deleterious effects upon subsequent achievement of growth and profit goals. A balance among areas is needed. If growth had not been sought, the problems would have been less serious. When sought, however, a consistency between the growth goal and other key areas was required.

Drucker's themes are logically attractive, have anecdotal evidence to support them, and have been used by a number of firms (Hassler, 1956). Cyert and March's (1963, p. 40) research based theory of organization supports the idea. They observe that "we can represent organizational goals reasonably well by using five different goals." These include a production, an inventory, a sales, a market standing and a profit goal. Cyert and March base the need for a theory of organizations to include the concept of multiple goals on the inability of managers to maximize profitability in the sense outlined by classical economic theory. The latter assumes perfect knowledge of prices, competitors' actions, and its own costs both now and in the future. Since these assumptions are unrealistic, as is well known, the classical economic theory of the firm is unable to predict prices or outputs or other behaviors of organizations in any accurate manner.

It should be noted that Cyert and March explain the emergence of multiple goals as emanating from members of a coalition powerful enough to force the organization to attend to these goals, rather than those emerging from top management. In the third chapter, attention will be given to those coalition and goal formation processes. While Learned and Sproat (1966) criticize the Cyert and March model as representing behavior in middle rather than top policy-level management, support for the concept of multiple goals is, at least, research based.

GOALS VS. CONSTRAINTS

It may be uncomfortable to think of multiple goals as ends toward which to direct an organization's activities. After all, what is served if the organization maximizes its management development activity? The reason that an enterprise considers management development worthy of attention and allocation of resources at all is that it provides some assurance of the long-run viability and effectiveness of the system. But as an organizational goal, management development could not stand on its own as an area for maximization. The development of managers may be a necessary condition or a constraint that needs to be satisfied rather than an end in itself. Simon (1964) contends that it is doubtful whether decisions are generally directed toward achieving *a* goal. Rather, a whole set of constraints constitutes the goal seeking ends. Therefore, the goal of organizational activity is to satisfy this set of constraints rather than to maximize the achievement of a single objective.

Constraints to the decisions made by a manager emerge primarily, according to Simon, from other parts of the organization rather than from the personal interests of the decision maker. An advertising manager is constrained in the amounts he will advertise by the capacity of the production facilities to provide articles for sale. He may also be constrained by a budget, but the capacity constraint may be, for a period of time, just as important in his decision behavior as is his budget. In a similar way, the advertising manager's decisions may be constrained by codes of ethics in the advertising profession, availability of different media types, product warranties, and characteristics, truth in advertising practices, and so forth. Although some of these constraints originate from above in the organizational hierarchy, others are created by decisions in other parts of the organization (for example, production capacity) or outside the legal boundaries of the firm (for example, laws regulating advertising).

The advertising manager considers production capacity a constraint, but he has incomplete knowledge of factory schedules and warehouse inventories for the products he advertises. He cannot directly couple advertising decisions to the production constraint, but the system is at least *loosely coupled* (Simon, 1964). Similarly, one of the measures that may be used to evaluate the advertising manager is gross margins produced per dollar of advertising. But since gross margins depend on product attractiveness, price, and other selling and promotion efforts, there can be a fairly wide range of acceptable values of the measure. The advertising system, then, is loosely coupled in a hierarchical, as well as a lateral, sense to decisions made elsewhere in the system.

GOALS OR CONSTRAINTS HAVE SIMILAR EFFECTS

Resources and attention are thus seen to be directed toward the achievement of either goals or constraints. Does it make any difference whether the area of concern is called a goal or a constraint, recognizing that the usual situation calls for attention to multiple criteria? Eilon (1971, p. 295) states that "constraints may be regarded as an expression of management's desire to have minimum attainments or levels of performance with respect to various criteria. *All constraints are, therefore, expressions of goals.*" While Cyert and March (1963, p. 40) discuss five different business goals, they summarize "that the goals of a business firm are a series of more or less independent constraints." Further, Simon (1964, p. 20) concludes: "Whether we treat all the constraints symmetrically or refer to some asymmetrically as goals is largely a matter of linguistic or analytic convenience." Thus, in the Drucker (1954) model, one could establish profitability or some measure of it as the main goal, and measures in each of the other seven key areas as constraints to be met. Such a formulation would allow the balance Drucker calls for. It would appear, however, that few decision changes would result because of this basically linguistic reformulation. It is possible to think of (1) achieving multiple goals or (2) meeting multiple constraints or (3) achieving a single goal under multiple constraints as equivalent formulations of the same decision problem.

WHY GOALS AREN'T ALWAYS MET

In classical economics, maximization of profits is the assumed goal of a business firm. The manager is "rational" insofar as his decisions have that maximizing effect. Deviation from maximization results in suboptimization. Suboptimization results in costs that can be measured, theoretically, by the difference between what occurred and what would have resulted from the optimum solution. In the classical economic model, suboptimization stems from irrational choices, since a correct decision from a rational manager would have resulted in the maximization of goal achievement. Thus, from the point of view of the firm, rationality is linked to optimization, and irrationality is linked to suboptimization. Similarly, rational optimizing behavior is "good" for society, because resources were used most efficiently in creating value. Conversely, irrationality and suboptimization are "bad," because resources are wasted.

SOURCES OF SUBOPTIMIZATION

In most organizations employing multiple objectives, the chances for suboptimization multiply greatly beyond those organizations devoted to a single goal. First, the objectives themselves may be in conflict, so that achievement of one is at the expense of one or more other goals. Line B in Figure 1.1 exemplifies the posited relationships when achievement of Y results in lesser performance on the X goal. Some inventors who start businesses to exploit one of their creations have become very successful in the market. When this occurs, the business requires plant, equipment, and working capital to produce and sell the expanding product volume. Yet, the business ordinarily will not create the profits and cash flows to finance the investments required from rapid growth. Thus, the firm is forced to enter the financial markets to obtain resources to support its success. If the entrepreneur also wishes to retain ownership control so that he may reap the benefits of his own creativity, he wants to avoid selling equity to outsiders. For some time, the firm can borrow until the growth requires a level of debt unacceptable to the lenders. At that time, slowing growth or giving up majority equity control are the primary alternatives remaining to the entrepreneur. Slow growth, however, invites competitors to enter and, if continued, could result in such a loss of market share that competitors would dominate the market. Such a market share scenario is also unacceptable to the entrepreneur who seeks to "reap the benefits" of his creation. High growth resulting from product success, retaining majority equity control, and reaping the benefits of the creative effort are, in fact, inconsistent goals for many highly "successful" small firms.

The inconsistency among goals is just as prevalent in large firms. Hatten and Schendel (1976) show that attempts to achieve higher market share by large national breweries has been at the expense of their profitability. The implications of their research for the strategic choice of goal levels of these firms is to maintain rather than increase market share, if such a goal is not to be inconsistent with achieving a profit goal. Of course, if these firms consider market share to be more important than profits, profits may be thought of as a constraint (which cannot be negative for long periods).

A set of goals may be complementary, as is shown in line A of Figure 1.1. Improving managerial capabilities through executive devel-

Figure 1.1 Types of Complementary Relations Among Goals

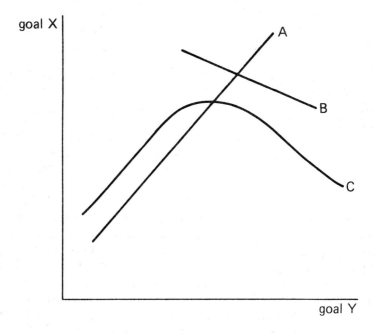

opment, for example, may be positively related to profitability. More likely, the relation resembles that of curve C, which indicates complementarity among goals at some levels of expenditure and inconsistency at other levels.

Although inconsistency among corporate objectives brings about suboptimization, the problem also arises because the goals of subparts of a system may interact in such a way as to have a deleterious impact upon overall goals. If the production department schedules long runs of parts to minimize its labor costs (a reasonable production goal among several), larger inventories of parts will be required. In turn, more inventory investment increases the investment base against which overall corporate profit is measured. Thus, by minimizing labor costs, return on investment could be adversely affected. If lowering labor costs does not result in increased profits sufficient to offset the rise in inventory investment, suboptimization with respect to the return on investment objective occurs.

The problem is analogous to attempting to apply optimizing management science models to a totality of operations of an organization. The problem is so large and complex that no computer can handle it.

Consequently, a partitioning of the overall into subproblems and the solution of each is made. When the subproblem solutions are added, however, their separate optimization fails to result in overall optimization of the decision.

SATISFICING VS. OPTIMIZING

In spite of the best available technology of management, then, suboptimization occurs. This results from the large scale of complexity in modern organizations. The sheer number of factors affecting an important decision places substantial informational and computational requirements upon the decision maker. Furthermore, there are often considerable time pressures on the manager to arrive at a decision quickly. There then is insufficient time to gather the required data even if it were available. As a consequence, the manager must and does act on less than full information. Rather than seeking all alternatives, he searches until there is a "satisfactory" solution, selecting the first available solution that meets his goals. If no satisfactory alternative is found, either additional search is undertaken or, ultimately, the objectives used are lowered so that one of the alternatives available fits within the revised criteria. If a salesman needs a new car for his job, and his search is unable to find one that meets all of his preestablished criteria, he may buy one without one of his requirements, for example, a differential traction transmission. He has not optimized, but the value of additional search, given his immediate need for a car, is not worth the result.

The above process is suboptimizing and irrational in the classical economic sense. Yet, it may be good management if time requirements and information costs are considered. March and Simon (1958) have labeled such a decision process as *satisficing* to distinguish it from maximizing behavior. Many scholars are uncomfortable with the satisficing concept, because they associate it with the bad connotations held about suboptimization. The classical economic model assumptions of complete knowledge, unlimited computational capacities, and knowledge of the probabilities of future events are unrealistic in large complex modern organizations. Satisficing decisions may be all that can be expected.

ORGANIZATIONAL
VERSUS PERSONAL GOALS

This book focuses upon goals of organizations. Although some authors contend that only people have goals and organizations reflect purposes sought by a collection of people, it is clear that organizations cannot satisfy all the goals of all its members. Many of us seek better health as a goal, yet few enterprises, other than health care organizations, directly service this personal goal. Many of us are also interested in greater personal affluence. If the organizations for which we work were to attempt to maximize all of our desires for personal affluence, they would soon become bankrupt.

Yet, organizations cannot ignore individual goals in their operation. They do provide rewards to individuals who can use the receipts to satisfy their personal needs. Indeed, some organizational activity can directly serve the goals of some individuals. A personal goal to achieve power and influence in the community may be possible by working for a political or governmental agency. A person starting his own business to meet a personal objective of employing his relatives can, if successful, exert enough power to achieve personal goals through organizational goals.

So far as personal are different from organizational goals, individuals pursuing their own ends create suboptimization.

EFFECTS OF GOAL
DIFFERENCES ON BEHAVIOR

Compare the differences in strategies and subgoals between two football teams with different overall goals: winning the Super Bowl versus a "rebuilding" year. A rebuilding team seeks to develop and give experience to younger players with potential for helping win in later years. In a rebuilding season, the team will sacrifice winning to provide game experience to rookies. It will trade proven veterans near retirement to acquire high potential draft choices. The emphasis is upon the future.

The team seeking to win the season's grand prize will use its best players. They will be withheld from play to allow lesser players opportunity only if injury, lack of the veteran's performance, or a big lead in the game warrants these substitutions. The plans for player acquisition, use of players in the game, attention in practice, and the set of actions constituting the team's strategy vary a great deal from those of a rebuilding team.

The two football teams have goals of substantially different *content*. They can be compared to two business firms, one with a primary objective of maximizing its profits and another seeking to increase its share of the market. Strategies and subgoals would be different for the two business firms, as well.

Even if the objectives of two organizations are similar, the way the goal is measured influences the supporting strategies and subgoals. A number of different measures or indicators of a goal can be used to transform it into a closed-end objective. Profit measures that are used include dollar amount, return on investment, earnings per share of stock, return on equity, and variations or combinations of these.

Sears Roebuck suffered relatively large declines in sales and profits in the 1974–1975 recession. Observers attributed Sears' failure to a strategic drift away from their traditional low to moderate price range. Store managers possessed the autonomy to select merchandise lines and were responsible for profits. To increase margins and thereby profits, store managers had tended to drop the lowest priced and lowest margin items. The effect was to reduce store traffic, particularly during recession periods. Less traffic meant that many potential buyers for high margin items were not drawn into the store in the first place.

To regain Sears' former position, its top management devised a new strategy consisting of centralization of authority and changes in goals. Store managers were made responsible for (1) sales, (2) profits in the store, and (3) profits in the region of which they are a part. The monetary bonuses of store managers were changed to reflect how well they had achieved these goals. Since revised compensation is based on sales as well as profits, store managers are more likely to carry and promote low priced items. Traffic and exposure to high margin items, thus, are seen as more likely. Managers will be less prone to overstock and hoard scarce items if other stores in their region can sell them, since managers' bonuses depend on regional profits.

The lessons to be learned from the Sears example are:

1. Corporate goals cannot be achieved without a consistent strategy. Organization structure, executive staffing, compensation system, and subgoals were all changed to the end of fitting them more closely with overall goals.

2. Managers attend to goals, particularly if they are paid and promoted to do so. Different goals elicit different behaviors. Even different measures of the same goal (profits in this case) change manager's actions.

3. Multiple goals for suborganizations are more likely to further corporate level objectives than a single one (profit for the store). At the same time, balancing multiple goals will make the store manager's task more complicated.

Table 1.1 compares the actions that can be taken to increase profits in a firm by the measure of profit used. Decreasing investments of and by itself will not increase profits *if they are measured by return on equity*, but it will increase return on investment. Conversely, increasing the amount of debt relative to stockholders' equity actually decreases profits, other things remaining the same, if profits are measured by *return on investment*. The same action increases profit if it is measured by *return on equity* and if overall profitability rates exceed interest rates on debt. A word of caution is that other things rarely remain the same. Nonetheless, the point to be emphasized is that different profit measures tend to elicit different strategies such as:

Profit Measure Maximized	Some Tendencies in Strategy
1. Earnings per share	1. Acquire firms with a lower price earnings ratio
2. Return on equity	2. Increase the relative proportion of debt in the financial structure
3. Return on investment	3. Increase sales and margins. Reduce investment per sales dollar

IDEALLY CONSTRUCTED GOALS

What is a good goal? Is there anything about their characteristics that would allow them to be more useful? There are two aspects of this question. One of them involves the nature of the goals themselves, that is, the content of the statements. A second aspect is the processes and conditions surrounding the establishment of the goals. Papers by Latham and Yukel (1975) and Hall (1977) reviewed the research literature providing support to the following concepts. Since there are a number of individual studies that analyze the characteristics of goals and goal setting, these two studies provide a starting point for more intensive investigation of these phenomena.

GOAL CONTENT

With respect to the content of the goal, *realistic* goals are more relevant toward influencing behavior than are those established on the basis of a whim. Although more difficult goals or goal levels have a

Table 1.1 Increasing Returns and Risks

Actions to Increase Returns	Risks
1. Decrease investment in *	
A. Cash	A. Ability to take cash discounts Decrease in credit worthiness
B. Receivables	B. Loss of credit as marketing tool
C. Fixed capital	C. Outmoded equipment, delivery and scheduling problems, inflexibility of operations
2. Increase sales volume	Overload plant Inventory outages
3. Increase prices selectively	Unit volume reduction Market share loss Experience curve loss
4. Decrease unit costs	lowered quality
5. Increase debt to equity ratio **	Inability to pay interest Lower returns on total investment

 * Does not necessarily apply to ROE, unless equity also is reduced.
** Applies to ROE, but not to Returns on Total Investment.

beneficial impact upon performance, the establishment of goal levels considerably in excess of anything yet achieved causes organizational participants to regard the goals as irrelevant and impossible. As a consequence, *difficult* but *achievable* goals have been stated as desirable. In this connection, also important is the *logical* arrangement of the stated goal with those of others. If a sales department is to provide sales volume at a 10 percent rate above the previous year while a second goal attempts to reduce the travel expenses of salesmen by 20 percent, the salesmen may have received two messages. One appears illogical in light of the other. The direction of behaviors expected is unclear. The clarity of goals is not only related to the logic of one goal in relation to the other, but it is also affected by the goal's statement and by its *specificity*. More general goals have less impact upon subordinate performance than specific ones. Yet, establishing specific, clear goals is not an easy process. In any event, clarity, logical consistency, realism, specificity, difficulty, and achievability are characteristics of goals toward which the manager should strive.

GOAL PROCESSES

In connection with the processes of establishing goals, management is most interested in the *acceptance* of these goals by subordinates. One of the major factors in whether a subordinate will accept a particular goal or goal level is the *commitment* to that goal by his superior. Thus, in establishing goals, the degree of top management and intermediate management commitment to these goals is highly important. If encouragement is not given to their achievement or if they are simply ignored by managers after establishment, little behavior change can be expected. Rather, encouragement of, constant attention to, and use of goals by superiors are seen as primary prerequisites to acceptance of goals by subordinates. To some extent, the training of managers in goal setting and in the use of goals can be useful in generating this commitment on their part to use them not only for themselves but for their subordinates.

The commitment of a manager toward a set of goals involves his *communication* of these goals to those with whom and over whom he works. This communication not only involves clarifying and stating these goals, but it also involves *feedback* of results and the use of controls relative to these goals. Feedback is a communication device as well as a means of control. Although participation in goal setting by subordinates has been successfully used to generate involvement and commitment to goal achievement on their part, successful goal systems have been established where participation was not used. An environment of *competition* is another factor that can add to goal achievement.

Thus, it is seen that the processes and conditions of the situation surrounding the use of goals is important in establishing acceptance of these goals by the individuals in an organization. If top management does not communicate its commitment to these goals through its statements and by its behavior, acceptance of the goals by lower-level individuals in the organization is unlikely to be pronounced. If cost cutting is established as a goal and management provides itself salary increases and perquisites, it is unlikely that subordinates will embrace the cost cutting goal. The atmosphere provided by top management in its commitment, its communication, its feedback, and in its training, together with establishing the competitive and expected behavior conditions are all influential in goal achievement.

Thus, both process and content affect goal achievement. Managers who wish to achieve the benefits of goal setting and goal processes in their organizations must consider the status and conditions of goals and the situation. These ideal conditions described above do not frequently exist in most organizations. As a matter of fact, the goal setting processes often are not ideal. It is the purpose of the third chapter to undertake a more thorough examination of the processes under which goals in an organization are established and achieved. This will provide a greater realism to the manner in which managers can, in fact, utilize goals in better administering their organizations. The next chapter sets the stage for this by examining the patterns of goals that exist and are effective in organizations.

SUMMARY

The purpose of this chapter was to introduce the study of goals and objectives. We found the following.

1. All organizations have goals. If there is no purpose, it makes no sense to organize in the first place.

2. Each goal can be either open or closed. Only closed goals are of much use in managing. Closed goals include:

    —a content
    —a measure or indicator
    —a level
    —a time period for achievement

3. Constraints and goals have much the same nature and effect in managing an enterprise.

4. Organizations do and should have multiple goals. Day to day maximizing of a single goal is usually dysfunctional in the long run.

5. A strategy is a series of actions, plans, programs, and so forth designed to achieve objectives. A strategy is the subsequent source of subgoals.

6. Goals are not maximized because of suboptimization and satisficing.

    —suboptimation occurs because of inconsistencies in goals at the same organizational level or between goals at lower levels inconsistent with those at higher levels.

—satisficing occurs because of lack of sufficient information and information processing to arrive at an optimal decision in the required time frame.

7. Different goals result in different managerial actions (for example, profit versus profits and sales in Sears).

8. Different measures of the same goal result in different managerial actions (for example, ROE versus ROI).

9. Criteria for goals include:

Good	Poor
clarity	vagueness
specific	general
logically consistent	inconsistent
difficult	easy
achievable	impossible

10. Ideal conditions for setting and achieving objectives include acceptance and motivation by subordinates achieved by:

—commitment to goals by the superior
—communication of goals
—feedback of results achieved toward goals
—competition among subordinates toward goal achievement

11. Managers achieve several purposes in using goals:

—planning the strategies is dependent on goals
—developing the organization structure and staffing it
—motivating and guiding subordinate behavior
—reviewing results achieved against plans provides the basis for control of organizational activities.

Since these purposes are the so called "managerial functions", of classical management theory, goals thus service all managerial behavior.

A couple of topics have been hinted at in this chapter:

1) there is a structured system of goals in an organization. The next chapter examines these phenomena.

2) personal as well as organizational goals exist. To what extent do they complement each other or conflict: How can personal goals interfere with organizational ones? This is covered in chapter three.

2

Goal Structures

In large-scale modern organizations, there are a wide variety of interrelated planning concepts and systems. There may be corporate missions; business charters; long-range plans; corporate policies; major programs; corporate creeds; grand designs; systems for programming, planning, and budgeting; capital investment systems; and so on. If such a mix of systems is not logically interrelated and if the sum total of the planning activities does not serve societal needs, the efficiency, effectiveness, and even the viability of the enterprise come to question. These ideas have been expressed by Urwick (1952, p. 10) as follows: "Unless we have a purpose there is no reason why individuals should try to cooperate together at all or why anyone should try to organize them."

HIERARCHY

One way of providing rationale and ordering of these many systems is through hierarchical placement (Simon 1969). Organisms as a whole consist of many subordinate parts, some of which are more important than others. The arm and hand are more important to overall functioning than the finger or fingernail. A complete organism consists of parts within subsystems nested within the whole. Major subparts existing within the human body include digestive, circulatory, locomotive, regulatory, and nervous systems. Parts of each system are nested within larger systems. Redundancy and interrelationships among systems exist. Some systems are higher in importance (for example, nervous and circulatory) to individual survival than others (reproductive or auditory).

The purpose of this section is to provide an explanation of the hierarchical arrangement of organizational goals. The discussion employs the concepts of nesting, importance, level, and interrelatedness to justify the logic of the ordering. Without such ordering, the logic of the network of plans is absent or not understood. Activities throughout a system can vary widely in effectiveness and efficiency. Without direction, effort tends to be pointed toward personal or professional goal achievement rather than organizational objectives.

ORGANIZATION STRUCTURE

It is obvious that most organization structures take on a hierarchical form. Structure is important, because the locus of planning, goal setting, and decision-making is dependent upon the type of structure in which the planning is done. Figure 2.1 presents a representation of two of the most prevalent kinds of organization structures. The hierarchical nature of goals and subgoals stems from organization hierarchy. Much of the planning that is performed at the product division level in the larger diversified organizations is performed at the corporate level in single product functionally organized organizations (Galbraith 1978). Additionally, there is a correspondence between the hierarchy of organization structure and the hierarchy of strategies. The engineering managers in charge of designing suspension systems for Ford Motor Company are not undertaking responsibilities to shape the master strategy of the corporation. Nor is Henry Ford II, chairman of the firm, intimately involved in the budgets, schedules, and assignments of personnel that are involved with a program to adapt automobile designs to accommodate radial tires. Each organization level could be viewed as having unique planning responsibilities and goals, although some systems obviously overlap several others.

REPRESENTING HIERARCHY

In chapter one, we noted that a goal structure could be represented by a matrix, with the goals at any level of organization being noted as a row in the matrix. Each row's goals supports objectives in the next

Figure 2.1 Dominant Corporate Organization Forms (Partial Representations)

A. Functional: for professionally managed single product line firms

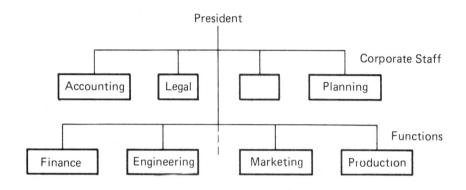

B. Product Divisionalized: for multi-product diversified firms

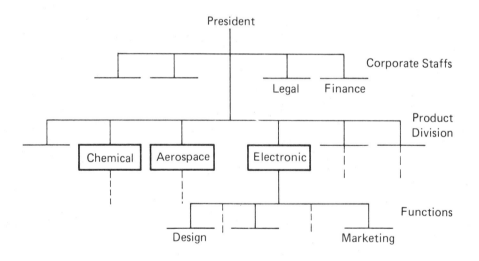

higher row in the matrix. While true, this idea is incomplete, since a goal at one level does not support all goals at the next level, only some of them.

A more accurate representation can be gleaned by examining Figure 2.2. Each goal is represented by an arch. Nested within the overall goal A are goals B and C. The B and C goals have no common subgoals. Thus, if goal F fails, it affects only B not C. The goals of B and C are interrelated only as they support A. If B fails, C is unaffected except as A is influenced.

E and F are supported by a common column. If column 3 fails, both E and F are first affected and then B to A, as explained above. The goals E and F interlock as do all D through G. This representation of hierarchy has been done with goals as the example. The same kind of explanation could be made for a hierarchy of strategies, managerial levels, or organization structure. Figure 2.2 is, in fact, analogous to the organizational structure of a product divisionalized firm as is shown in Figure 2.1. A can be likened to a corporate goal. Then, B and C would be goals for different product divisions. Goals D through G would represent functional goals for product division B, and goals H through K would represent functional goals for product division C.

The commonalities of hierarchy for organization, management, goals, and strategy are shown in Table 2.2. The table was prepared to summarize the analysis of this chapter, but it might be useful to examine it at this point to preview what is coming and the interrelationships among these parts.

Figure 2.2 Representing Hierarchy

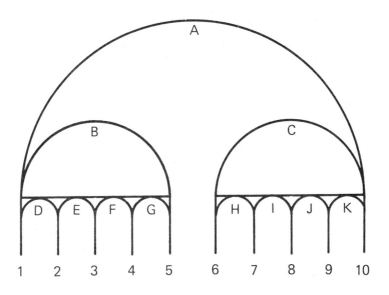

HIERARCHY OF OBJECTIVES

At the highest level, that of legitimacy, social institutions are sanctioned, encouraged, and constrained by the larger society of which they are a part. The system of private property ownership in the United States is sanctioned and encouraged because of the proposition that systems of public ownership of the means of production and distribution of goods and services are not as consistent with the fundamental concepts of freedom of individual choice and efficiency as private enterprise is. The totality and the individual units of private enterprise are expected to contribute to furthering the goals of society. Since, however, there often are unintended dysfunctional consequences of any activity, society constrains activities of its organizations to minimize undesired effects. Pollution standards are established; discrimination in employment is forbidden; hours of work are regulated, and so on.

GUIDING PHILOSOPHY

Within the framework of sanctions, encouragement, and constraints imposed by society as a whole, the contributions that a particular organization may want to make and the way it will operate to make them can be established. A high fashion dress manufacturer may want to bring excitement, uniqueness, and flair to its customers rather than protection and warmth. Custom designed dresses are considered means of satisfying these intended values. The managerial beliefs of what is important are integral at this level. If the motto "Progress is our most important product" guides the behavior at General Electric, it is more than an advertising program; it is an expressed value that governs and influences. Crown Cork and Seal has enunciated its beliefs, including: "A business enterprise does not exist solely for the benefit of any one group, neither customers, nor stockholders, nor employees, nor public, but that the benefits for all groups must be in balance and that the resulting benefits are the products of a well-run business" (Higginson 1956, p. 17).

Organizational philosophy may be codified in the form of creeds that state the principles, beliefs, and important values to which the organization ascribes. Corporate creeds often sound moralistic and close to the principles of free enterprise, as they well might since it is at the philosophical level that the relation between the firm's intellect and that of society's is closest. Indeed, if the White House under President Nixon had followed precepts more closely aligned with those originally developed in the U.S. Constitution, Watergate and its subsequent consequences would more likely have been avoided.

Although admirable creeds may be developed, if they are not followed or are contravened, leadership has failed. Under such circumstances, the legitimacy of the institution comes into question in larger society, as philosophies are viewed as window dressing rather than reality. Gulf Oil and Lockheed replaced their chief executive officers, primarily because the guiding philosophies under which the companies were actually operating (rather than those that may have been published) were at odds with societal expectations. The activities of these (and other) firms have, in the opinion of other business peers, brought into question the ability of free enterprise to function for society in the intended manner. This fear of commercial intentions is reflected by the routine of a comedian who paired incongruous word combinations. One pair that received a laugh was "business ethics." In spite of (and perhaps because of) Watergate, Gulf, Lockheed, and so forth, there are a number of firms whose concern for guiding philosophy and principles is based on the premise that without insuring itself of a match between its values and beliefs with those of society, it risks additional constraints from society as well as questions as to the legitimacy of the firm from within.

CORPORATE GOALS

At the overall corporate level, objectives of publicly held firms are stated most frequently in financial terms. Sales and sales growth, profit and profit growth, cash flow, earnings per share and its growth, coupled with dividend payment policy, stock appreciation, maintenance of major stockholder control, and so on are the areas in which corporate goals have been established. In addition to financial goals whose contents and level are of most interest to stockholders and corporate managers, whose compensation may be dependent on them, corporate-level goals may also address objectives of interest to other legitimate constituencies of the enterprise. At least one firm stated as its overriding goal: "To maximize the satisfaction of our employees." Profit was only considered as a constraint, enough being sought to keep the firm solvent. Major attention was given to providing comfortable, unstressful, participative, enjoyable work surroundings. The company was so successful in achieving employee satisfaction that it almost went broke.

Goals of organizations closely controlled by a few stockholders may reflect the personal objectives of their owners. The overriding objective of the entrepreneur in one retail store was to leave an inheritance to his children.   Tax laws severely constrained his inheritance goal, so that the form and operation of the business were altered considerably from what would have happened if he merely sought to maximize profits by attention to the owner's goal and the I.R.S. constraints.

Even in publicly held firms, the importance that top management may place on certain values often will emerge as corporate goals. Dr. Land, who founded Polaroid Corporation, has been observed to seek technologically difficult product development and sale as much as profits.   Thus, personal values at times emerge as corporate ends to be achieved.

Another dimension to corporate goals is attention given to other stockholders in the fruits of the system.   Some, such as unions or governmental agencies, impose constraints on the enterprise as a whole.   These constraints are attended to, require resources, and need to be balanced just as any other goal, as we noted in chapter one.   In still other areas, such as equal opportunity employment, the firm may exercise discretion in advance of governmental imposition of goals to establish its own objectives in that area.

CORPORATE NONFINANCIAL GOALS

Diversified multi-product firms are of two types (Pitts 1977).   For firms that have diversified by acquiring other firms through tender offers, mergers, and similar tactics—in popular terminology, the conglomerates—top corporate management maintains a relatively small staff consisting primarily of financial planning and control experts. As a consequence, the diversified firms that have become that way through acquisition tend to establish only financial criteria for planning and control of the several product divisions.

In contrast, large multi-product firms that have diversified through internal research and development tend to have rather large corporate staffs that include the same type of financial experts as the conglomerates but that also include staffs in the functional areas important to the operation of the firm.   General Electric and Westinghouse are prototypes of internally diversified firms.   Internal diversifiers tend to establish corporatewide objectives for research and development, managerial resources, physical resources, and so on.   In fact, at one time General Electric used the eight key areas in which results should be expected as proposed by Drucker (1954).   Thus, establishing corporate goals in an internally diversified multi-product firm is much more complex, in that the process involves a broader range of objectives to be established.

CORPORATE BALANCE IN OBJECTIVES

Multiple objectives need to be set and balanced with each other to remove potential inconsistencies among them. The following example uses only financial criteria, but similar analyses could be made for other kinds of goals. Closed corporate goals cannot be established independently of each other. Consider only two goals:

—4 percent increase in sales volume per year for ten years
—15 percent increase in profits per year for ten years

Unless there are remarkable economies of scale or terribly inefficient past operations, the profit increases seem high relative to the sales goal. For most businesses, these two goals would be incompatible. A sustained five or six percent increase in profits per year, given a four percent sales growth, might approach a reasonable balance.

Not only do overall goals need to be consistent with each other, they also need to be consistent with the master strategy of the firm. The master strategy supposedly follows from corporate goals as a means of accomplishing them. For an established organization, it is not easy to change the master strategy very quickly, although it can be done over time. If 15 percent per year return on investment after taxes is set as a major objective, and the master strategy has placed the firm in forest products, then corporate goal and master strategy inconsistencies appear to exist. Forest product companies have rarely, if ever, been able to approach a 15 percent return on investment. The goal is unrealistic in light of the master strategy.

Of course, it is possible to alter a master strategy. Selling off the forest products business to enter other lines of products or services would typify such a change. The ability to alter a master strategy depends a great deal upon the flexibility in use of the managerial, financial, and physical resources of the firm. If these timberlands are readily salable, strategic alterations would be easier than if they were not marketable resources.

The process of setting goals, establishing strategies, then reevaluating goal levels, and readjusting strategies occurs from the top to the bottom. Accommodation of strategy to goals and vice versa provide management the means to integrate operations at all levels to objectives sought at overall levels.

MASTER STRATEGY

The grand design of a firm in the form of its master strategy is a visionary projection of the central and overriding concepts on which the organization is based.   Henry Ford envisioned the "people's car" and embodied this central concept into a business strategy that resulted in the Model T Ford.   If the railroads had not been in the "railroad business" (Leavitt 1960) but had stated a master strategy in the form of: "To provide rapid, safe, low cost transportation of goods and people at intercity distances", they may have been able to thrive and prosper by entering airline, truck, bus, and barge modes of transportation.   This statement of master strategy would have kept them out of urban mass transport and overseas shipping, but it would have prevented the tunnel vision and the resulting overconcentration on a particular, limited mode of transport.   It would have allowed consideration of alternate business strategies that encompassed other means of accomplishing the basic need for transportation.

A master strategy, then, should not focus on what the firm is doing in terms of products and markets currently served, but rather upon the services and utility that their products provide.   A vacuum tube performs certain functions in amplification and conversions of electrical current.   By focusing attention upon tubes rather than the functions they provide, the vacuum tube manufacturers were outflanked by semiconductor firms that ultimately provided lighter, smaller, more reliable, and cheaper means of providing the same functions.   Cooper and Schendel (1976) found that during technological change, companies that were leaders in the old technology were rarely leaders in the new one.   In contrast to this research, however, I.B.M., a leader in punch card technology, became the dominant computer manufacturer.   If the old I.B.M. is viewed as providing means for data manipulation rather than as leasing tabulating equipment, the transition to computers, typewriters, software systems, and office copiers becomes more understandable.   The role of the master strategy is to provide a basis of the firm's unique position for competition using existing products and markets.   At the same time, the master strategy provides flexibility of outlook for the creative efforts of individuals in the organization to seek new and expansive methods through new products, new systems, and new customer groups. Thus, a master strategy ought to provide a conceptual framework for renewal and growth.

To be viable over long periods, the master strategy also must be viable in the light of environmental conditions.   While Granger (1964, p. 68) reports a successful master strategy of a firm making seals as "to stop the leaks of the world," it is doubtful that a hat firm seeking "to cover and protect the heads of American men" would prove as viable. Until recently, the American male has increasingly been going hatless. Providing a service that is becoming obsolete because of changing tastes and habits is inconsistent with environmental conditions. Yet, predicting the environmental viability of a master strategy over time is extremely hazardous. Who can predict that a new cheap plastic cannot be developed and produced to be used in stopping leaks under a wide variety of conditions of pressure, temperature, corrosion, and so on? This question raises the more general question of, How permanent are any set of needs in society? While nutrition, health, and other needs appear basic, the form of technology and products to service them can and has changed over time.

Rather than the utility and service basis for a master strategy, some firms have successfully relied upon a technology that has many applications. Corning Glass Works has extensive technical expertise in glass technology that can be used in a wide variety of products serving a variety of consumer and industrial requirements. Although strategies based upon a single technology (for example, the steam locomotive) are subject to risk as technology changes, an extensive technology with a variety of products serving many needs is less subject to such risk. General Motors' master strategy has as its core the exploitation of motors energized by liquid hydrocarbons (Sloan 1964). Although this scheme has generated substantial success, its future is clouded by the potential shortages of hydrocarbons. In the late 1970s, it might appear that a master strategy based upon a glass rather than a hydrocarbon motor technology would be more consistent with environmental conditions.

A logical master strategy must not only be consistent with environments but also the internal capabilities of the organization. A strategy "to provide safe, low cost means of personalized air transport for personal and business use" appears consistent with the design, production, and marketing capabilities of Piper Aircraft. Conversely, a statement "to provide vehicles for above ground or sea transport" is a much broader statement that could imply military, space, and airline transport products. Since the functional requirements of such vehicles are so different from the capabilities inherent in providing light aircraft, the master strategy for a company employing such a statement would appear rhetorical and pompous, rather than a realistic guide to the products and services that Piper could reasonably hope to offer. Too broad a statement of a master strategy runs the risk of being inconsistent with capabilities. Too narrow a statement runs the risk of being made obsolete by changing environmental technology, tastes, customs, and laws.

MASTER STRATEGY
AND BUSINESS GOALS

It is at the level of a separate line of business, the business unit level, that corporate management will be interested in establishing multiple objectives. In chapter one, it was noted that Drucker (1954) proposes eight key areas in which results expected should be established if long-run success is to be achieved: market standing, innovation, productivity, physical and financial resources, profitability, manager performance and development, worker performance and attitude, and public responsibility. Each business unit would develop separate and different levels of results to be achieved and different time frames within which to accomplish them. In other words, although the open-ended goals might be similar for each business unit, the closed-end objective would differ from one line of business to another.

The goals from each business are expected to contribute to overall goals and the implementation of the master strategy. One firm's master strategy included the policy that only high quality products would be produced. In one corporate acquisition, the company received a product line that was sold on a price basis and had one of the lowest quality levels in the industry. An immediate objective set for the business was to achieve the highest quality level of all major competitors. This corporate policy generated not only a quality goal but also necessitated changes in the plans and policies of the acquired business to make its strategy consistent with the corporate goal of quality.

EFFECTS OF DIVISION
STRATEGY ON ITS GOALS

Although each product division is expected to contribute to corporate goals, each does so differently.

In an aging line of business near the end of its product life cycle, the goal for physical resources might reasonably be to reduce overall investments by 10 percent (exclusive of depreciation) during the next year. For a business unit experiencing rapid growth, however, the next year's physical resource goal might be to add capacity to take care of projected sales for the next three years.

The point to be made is that the goals of a business unit are supposedly developed from overall corporate strategy. Then, the business strategy is developed from its goals. It is the contention, here, however, that business goals set without reference to the business strategy, or variations of it that could be established, may result in a mismatch between the goals and the strategy. The same point was made with respect to corporate goals and master strategy by the forest products firm. The top down approach to (1) establishing goals and then (2) establishing strategy most often does not stop there. After a strategy is developed, it is evaluated to see whether it can, in fact, meet the goals previously set. If it could exceed them, the goals tend to be readjusted upward. If it cannot meet preestablished goals, the goals may be readjusted downward. This process of setting goals, establishing strategy, reevaluating goals and then strategy continues in a cascading fashion until consistent agreement between the two is reached.

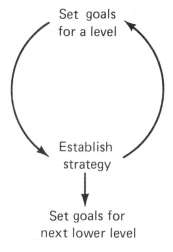

Since the power of corporate executives tends to be relatively high, division general managers tend to be pushed toward achieving ever higher levels of results. For some types of businesses, this is realistic. For others, it is not. A number of models for the development of business-level strategies have been created. Hofer and Schendel (1978) in this West Series on Policy and Planning provide an explanation and evaluation of them. Most are multi-factored models, but the following is a simpler two-dimensional model. It is offered as a way of explaining how different businesses can be positioned strategically to meet their goals.

BCG MODEL

The Boston Consulting Group (Henderson 1968) has used the following model extensively with its clients in their choice and use of product/market strategy. The concept of the experience curve underlies part of the reasoning for the model. The experience curve idea can be stated as follows: "For a given product design, the value-added costs of production are reduced by a fixed percentage each time the cumulative unit production is doubled." This definition conceals as much as it reveals. A "given product design" means that the cost reduction occurs only as design remains constant. Any change in product design puts the firm on a new learning curve. When I.B.M. changed from magnetic cores to integrated circuits in the design of its computer memories, the experience in making magnetic cores was lost except as that experience could be transferred to integrated circuit memories. Thus, a change in product design involves a different experience curve. Integrated circuits were selected, ultimately because their potential costs were lower and performance characteristics higher. Hopefully, a company can select a product design that will lower costs and put them on an experience curve that is substantially lower than that on which they have already had experience.

In the definition of the experience curve, "value-added" means that raw material costs are not subject to cost reduction effects. (Purchased subassemblies, however, should have experienced-based cost reductions.) The experience curve definition implies that every time production is doubled, the unit costs, as defined above, go down a fixed percentage. In assembly work, the reduction typically is in the neighborhood of 20 percent. Thus, if the value-added costs of production of the first unit were $100, the cost of production of the second unit would be 80 percent of that, or $80, the fourth unit $64, and so on. The costs are often represented as a straight line on a log-log scale such as line C in Figure 2.3.

Pricing

The implications of a constantly lowering unit cost of production as the cumulative experience increases has strategic implications. In order to achieve costs lower than competitors, greater cumulative experience would be helpful. This implies that the most successful firm, the one with the dominant cost structure, would be that firm that has the most cumulative experience. To gain cumulative experience, it is necessary or certainly helpful to have a high market share of the product in the total market. The ability to attain high market share is, in turn, highly dependent on the prices that the individual firm places on its product. In Figure 2.3, line P_1 illustrates the pricing strategy of bringing prices down to match the cost levels obtained under the experience curve. For a firm entering early into a market area, such pricing strategy makes entry less attractive for competitors. Conversely, line P_2 presents a skimming pricing tactic. This skimming approach is somewhat dangerous as it allows competitors to enter under the high price umbrella, until they themselves can gain the experience to reduce their costs along the experience curve. In fact, if one firm is to price by a skimming approach while its competitor is using a cost-based pricing approach, the latter firm should increase its market share and lower its cost to such an extent that it would be very difficult for the skimming firm to remain viable.

Figure 2.3 The Experience Curve

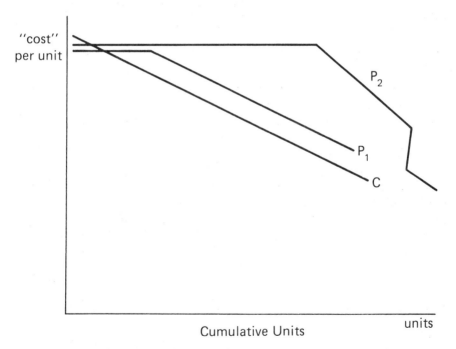

"cost" per unit

P_2

P_1

C

Cumulative Units

units

C = value added

P_1 = Cost pricing tactic

P_2 = Price skimming tactic

A log-log scale is used

Growth-Share Matrix

Translating experience curve concepts into market share and relating the market share of the firm to the overall growth of the market results in a growth-share matrix as shown in Table 2.1. A firm with a low market share in a low growth market would be one for which the total market had reached maturity, that is, the product is at the end of its product life cycle. Firms that had very low market shares at that point would not have achieved the necessary cumulative units of experience to allow them to have a competitive cost structure with other firms that had high market shares. Therefore, this kind of firm would be marginally profitable, at best, and is characterized by BCG as a "dog." Alternatively, organizations with high market shares have relatively low cost structures since their cumulative experience is high. An example of this sort of firm in the automobile industry is General Motors. Most of its plants and facilities have been built. It does not require large increases in working capital and fixed investments in order to maintain its market share, and its costs of production are low. Under such circumstances, the business would generate more cash than it would need. BCG characterizes such firms as "cash cows." The cash flows can be used to fund new businesses or to pay high dividends. In comparison with General Motors, American Motors could probably be considered the "dog" of the automobile industry. It has lost money as often as it has made it in recent years. It has been marginally profitable in the automobile portion of its business, where it has a relatively low, that is, less than 5 percent, market share.

In contrast are companies in markets that are growing relatively rapidly, that is, firms whose business is in the early stages of the product life cycle. A business that has a large market share in a growth market can be characterized as a "star," since if it continues to experience high market share, rapid progess down the learning curve, and increasingly lower costs, it will eventually turn into a cash cow when the market matures. During growth, it requires large amounts of working capital and fixed investments to produce and sell its products while maintaining high market share. In a sense, the "star" is also a cash hog. Although a star may be extremely profitable, substantial cash inputs are nevertheless required to provide the facilities for the star to maintain its growth in a growing market.

The final category of firms is the "question marks," those firms with low market shares in high market growth fields. If the business does not obtain larger market shares, it will never experience the cost reductions that its more successful competitors, will, and it

Table 2.1 Growth-Share Matrix

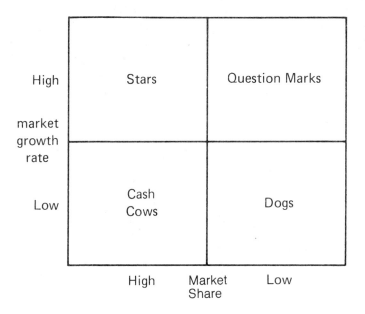

will ultimately become a dog. The strategic choice is whether or not the firm is willing to raise the capital in order to move the "question mark" to a position of higher market share, so that it may become a star (and ultimately a cash cow) rather than to await the maturity of the market and become a dog.

BUSINESS STRATEGIES
AND BUSINESS GOALS

How does the BCG model modify our thinking about business goals? How does this information feed back upon the results setting process at the business level? First, the output from a business changes over time. A high share business in infancy becomes profitable as it becomes a star, and more so as it matures. Its cash flow is negative during growth and positive during maturity. Different goals for the same business at different times should be normal.

Secondly, each of the several product divisions in a diversified firm will likely be in a different position in the growth-share matrix, so that different expectations of their results should be evident. The same growth rates and profit rates for all businesses cannot be expected.   To fine tune business goals, then, consideration both from the master strategy and from the business's strategic position is relevant.

If an organization has one product line classified as a star and another as a cash cow, the firm is fortunate, because both can contribute to overall strategy.   The cow, however, ordinarily would be assigned the goal of furnishing a net cash inflow to corporate coffers. The cash would then be distributed to the star, whose goals would be modified to seek growth in size, perhaps market share, and certainly resources.

The role of those managing the master strategy is to juggle the individual businesses the strategy has to manage to insure that overall corporate level goals are met.   Each line of business can best contribute in different ways.

Functional Goals

Large-scale group endeavors require division of efforts, so that each part of the job required to accomplish overall goals can be performed more efficiently.   At some level of most organizations, a functional organization form is found.   The grouping consists of individuals assigned a common specialized task on the basis of the kind of work performed.   Examples of functional organizations are engineering, production, marketing, finance, and manufacturing.   In a retail store, the functions are buying, inventory, stock control, display, selling, credit, and delivery.   In a multi-product firm, there may be separate parallel functional organizations.   For example, a company producing pumps, motors, and valves might have separate engineering organizations for each of these products as well as separate production and marketing organizations.

The goals of each functional department are fashioned by the nature of its environment, which not only consists of societal expectations, but also the strategy of the business that it is a part of.   In addition, the environment of any particular department, such as engineering, is constrained or influenced by the activity and goals of other functional organizations with which it interacts.   Most frequently, these interactions occur at the same organizational level and within the same product line of business.   For example, in a company producing pumps, motors, and valves, the engineering organization designing valves may be little influenced by the production or marketing organizations working with pumps.   But within the valve division itself, the engineering of the valves, the preciseness of engineering standards, and the relevance of these standards to the operation of the valve greatly influence the ability of the manufacturing department to produce and assemble these valves so that they will work.

Thus, if the engineering department provides a very rough engineering design, the manufacturing department would spend considerable time adjusting and filing down parts, forcing assemblies, and so on, in order to make the valve parts fit together and work properly. Whether the engineering department should attempt to achieve preciseness in design depends to some extent on the overall business strategy and the goals of the marketing department, as well. If a design is expected to sell in large volumes over long periods of time, the engineering department could be expected to expend much time and energy in engineering, drafting, pilot and experimental productions, and testing before the finalized design is sent to manufacturing for large-scale production. On the other hand, if the valve is specially ordered and will only be produced once, the amount of engineering time that would be economical to devote to the valve would be relatively less, even though such a design would require more adjustments in production. Thus, the functional goal of degree of preciseness of design for an engineering department depends upon its constraints and relationship to other departments, that is, marketing and production, as well as to the overall objectives of the valve business itself. If general management is developing the business as a specialized valve manufacturer, the goals of the production, marketing, and engineering departments would be considerably different than if a mass market strategy were being pursued.

Although the functional organization's goals are dependent upon those of the parent business and other functional units with which it interacts, the importance of different functions varies by the particular partitioning of the business in the growth-share matrix. If, for example, the valve business is classified as a question mark, and if the business decision is to attempt to move the business to a star position, the marketing department's strategy under such an overall business strategy would involve considerable promotion, selling effort, advertising, and so on, in order to achieve an increased market share goal. Thus, the relevant importance of marketing under these conditions would be rather high compared to what it would be if the firm were classified as a dog.

If the product is a dog, the business may be attempting to find a particular market niche in which it can become dominant. It would wish to avoid direct competition with industry leaders but to remain in the business by finding an area of it in which the leaders do not compete. At one time, for example, American Motors was attempting to distinguish itself from the three big car manufacturers by focusing upon small cars while the big three were pursuing large car sales. Under such a product differentiation mode, the firm attempts to avoid head-on competition with leaders. It focuses its advertising upon groups of customers whose needs are met by the differentiated product, and its resources are differentiated rather than the same as competitors. The goals of the engineering department are to design a different small car rather than a better big car. Goals and the requirements for behavior within functions are different, then, depending on how the business involved is positioned in the growth-share matrix and the strategic choices made about that position.

SUMMARY

This section has shown that a *single* goal does not very well represent the kinds of objectives that organizations actually seek. Rather, organizations, both their parts and their total, each seek multiple goals. Their objectives and subobjectives are influenced by the larger system of which they are a part (See Table 2.2). Overall guiding principles and the master strategy of the firm are the links that the firm has to society as a whole. These links fashion the overall objectives of the organization. Particular kinds of business have separate and differentiated goals that are based upon its stages in the product life cycle or upon its position in the growth-share matrix. Functional goals are dependent upon the objectives and the type of business in which the organization of which it is a part is undertaking. Furthermore, functional objectives, as the objectives of any other unit in an organization, are dependent on and constrained by the activities and goals of other units with which it interacts. Inconsistency among goals at a particular organizational level and friction among subsystems exist because of a lack of clarity about how behavior in one subsystem affects that in others. There is an imperfect mesh among the goals of functional departments. This inconsistency may require a constant adjustment of goals and constraints as each system mutually interacts with others.

Goal structures of a unit are influenced not only vertically from above and below, but also in a horizontal or lateral sense by the constraints and goals of other units with which it interacts.

RELEVANCE OF GOAL STRUCTURES

What does all this mean to the manager? How can he use it? Several conclusions can be drawn.

In complex organizations, several distinct but interrelated hierarchies exist:

—goal hierarchy
—strategy hierarchy
—managerial hierarchy
—organizational hierarchy

Table 2.2 shows the correspondence of these levels. In addition, it shows the flow between goals and strategies at different levels. As we have previously mentioned, strategy at any one level feeds back in a cascading maneuver to the goals at that level. To show that reverse feedback effect, the arrows in Table 2.2 would need to have their reverse shown as well.

In addition to vertical hierarchies, there are horizontal relationships among goals, strategies, managers, and organizational units at any one level. At the general manager of an autonomous product division level, the horizontal relationships to other product divisions in the corporation often are not very important and do not need much coordinated effort. (This would be modified if buying and selling between divisions was common.) At the functional level of the organization, however, the goals and strategies of any function affect every other and tend to interlock. As noted, the goals at the functional level do and must be interrelated. At least, goals of other interlocking functions constitute constraints.

Looking vertically, then, a manager wants to assure himself that his strategy is consistent with his goals and that his goals best service the strategies of his superior. In the downward direction, he uses his subordinates' goals as indicators of how well he can carry out his strategy. Thus, coordination of their efforts through negotiating their goals (and often advising on their strategies) is required.

Looking horizontally, a manager needs to assure himself that his goals are consistent with those of others, to the extent they interact. Functional managers most often find this a problem and will be resolved in many instances by self-coordination with other managers. The superior of several interdependent units, however, also needs to assure himself that subordinate goals and strategies are designed to mesh in a coordinated manner.

Table 2.2 Goal Structures and Hierarchy

Organizational Hierarchy	*Managerial Hierarchy*	*Goal Hierarchy*	*Strategic Hierarchy*
Board of Directors Corporate Offices	Founder, Chairman, President	Economic and social values and balance among them ⟶	Guiding Philosophy
Corporate	President	Overall goals corporate objectives ⟷	Master Strategy
Business Unit and corporate	President; Division Manager	Business goals ⟷	Business Strategies
Functions and Business unit	Function Manager;	Functional Goals ⟵	Functional Strategies

3

Politicized Goal Setting Processes

RATIONAL PROCESSES

The last chapter showed the relationships among goals and strategies at various levels in a multi-product firm. In addition to establishing objectives and strategies, an organizational unit also may engage in long-range planning and yearly planning or budgeting. In a rational top-down relationship among these several systems, the following diagram may be helpful.

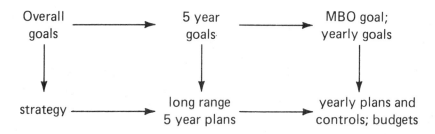

Overall goals are a basis for development of strategy and for establishing what long-range goals should be accomplished within a particular time frame. Five years has been used as the interval for long-range planning because that is typical for U. S. organizations, although longer and shorter periods are not uncommon. During the five-year period, the overall goal represents a target at which the five-year-goals aim. The overall organizational goal might state a 12 percent return on investment, and a five-year plan might seek intermediate levels of return on investment to get from where the firm is actually operating to where its overall goals and grand design dictate.

Long-range plans constitute a set of activities to couple strategy to present operations. Both the establishment of strategy and its implementation through long-range planning and goals are the subject of chapter five. A yearly budget and goals for the short range stem from long-range plans. MBO as an approach to couple current expected results to longer-range goals is the topic of chapter six.

In a completely rational system, overall goals are closely linked to overall strategy and the goals of a long-range planning system. In those enterprises facing a highly uncertain environment, the ability and the desirability of a tight coupling among these elements is questionable. Thus, different organizations might link them together more or less closely, depending upon the predictability of the conditions faced.

Similarly, MBO goals and the yearly plans may actually constitute a higher specification of activity during the nearest year in a five-year plan. In contrast to such a tight coupling, some MBO goal setting and yearly budgeting are developed with less reference to the long-range planning. The reason for such looseness in coupling may stem from a lack of experience in integrating from strategic goals to MBO systems. Another reason may be the disbelief that planning can be usefully translated in the firm to operationally viable action plans.

The connection between goals and operations in the systems described above is understandably rational in intention. The overall purposes are served through the conscious development of an interrelated series of plans and objectives. Although some firms can and do approach such behavior, the complexity of large-scale organizations, together with the personal desires and interests of individuals in groups, make the task of achieving rational, optimal goals difficult. Managers who do consider optimality desirable are frustrated in achieving it. It is the purpose of this chapter and the next to review some of the major findings of research directed toward a better understanding of the political rather than rational goal setting processes. With this knowledge, managers can deal with the establishment of goals more realistically in light of the behavioral and political processes that exist in organizations (MacMillan 1978).

POWER

To accomplish this task, it is first important to recognize that power, or the ability and willingness to influence affairs in an organization, and the values held by individuals and groups can directly influence goal formation and achievement. Because the distribution of power is sometimes widespread rather than concentrated, attention to goals emanating from a number of individuals within and external to the organization may be required. The resolution of disjointed interests leads to a number of social interactions affecting the character and means for achieving objectives. Yet, certain patterns of goal groupings have been discovered. It is to these patterns that the manager turns his attention if he chooses to use and influence the goal processes of his organization.

POWER SOURCES

Every individual possesses some degree of power. The president of a large corporation may have far-ranging influence upon its direction and activity. The janitor may have only the power to perform tasks as assigned or to refuse to do so, risking the potential consequences of his choice. Since any member can be replaced at some cost to the system, individual power is restricted. The range of power discretion among different individuals is obviously great.

Potential ability to influence is not always used in totality. The president may have the power to insist that the marketing vice-president and the marketing organization focus their activities on the goal of increasing product market share 10 percent per year over the next three years. In fact, the president may elect not to insist on such a goal, preferring that the marketing group participate with him in establishing its objectives. Potential power is not always exercised. Since power limits are somewhat fuzzy, it may be dangerous to employ one's full powers and then risk failure. The dean of a professional school in a large university, attempting to demonstrate his support, asked his faculty for a vote of confidence. When, instead, a vote of no confidence resulted, an observer noted that the dean had overestimated his limits of power to rally support.

One of the useful frameworks for discussing power sources is the French and Raven (1959) paper widely cited in this regard. They distinguish five bases of social power: reward, coercive, referent, expert, and legitimate sources. The ability to influence by providing rewards for desired behaviors constitutes the *reward* basis. Many forms of organizational rewards (for example, pay, prestige, position, perquisites, and status) may increase the influence of the individual controlling these rewards.

Coercive power stems from the ability of an individual to influence another through punishment or threat thereof. Carrying through on threats, if behavior is unacceptable, is as important as carrying through in providing promised rewards if power is not to be eroded or lost. Since coercive threats are considered repressive to some, the use of coercive means to influence others may not be used as extensively in some societies as in others.

Referent power is the ability to influence that an individual has because of the identification another has with him. John F. Kennedy was able to attract members to his administration because of the aura of personality he exuded. Identification provides the individual with a means to incorporate, psychologically, the strength of another in himself. Whether objectives to which a leader ascribes are a precondition to his obtaining referent power or whether goals are established by him after achieving power is open to question. For example, Winston Churchill, the great World War II leader, lost the election after his cause was won. Certainly, the influence of great causes and charismatic leaders go together. In any event, a manager may have numerous individuals that want to identify with him because he demonstrates admired characteristics. To the extent that a manager or leader enjoys this condition, he is able to exert referent power. Few leaders are able freely to create a charismatic condition favorable to them, however.

Expert power refers to the potential of one to influence another because of superior knowledge and expertise in a particular field. The acceptance of a consultant's recommendations stems from his unique experience-based abilities. Growing knowledge and complexity prevents comprehensive knowledge of organizations and their operations. Thus, modern organizations rely on experts and expertise as a power source tends to increase. A statement that "this pump will not stand up in the field under the corrosive conditions of its potential uses" will not have much influence if it comes from the advertising director with no expert knowledge of the subject. Influence to change the decision would be greater if it came from someone acquainted both with conditions and the resistance of the materials used, such as an engineer or designer.

A final base of social power in the French and Raven framework is *legitimacy*. An individual accedes to the suggestions of others, because he perceives it is correct that he do so. Legitimate power in organizations is associated with the position the individual occupies. Because he is the boss, a new salesman follows the lead of his district sales manager. At the same time, the salesman may not be influenced by suggestions from the chief accountant whose position is not considered as a legitimate source of power over the salesman. Even individuals closely associated with a legitimate power can influence others, as one can observe that a call from the president's secretary gets as much attention as one from a respected associate.

COALITION FORMATION

Because there are diverse bases for social power in organizations, managers are able to influence others from multiple power sources. At the same time there are competitive individuals and managers with power in the hierarchy above, beside, and below him. If power is relatively evenly and widely dispersed, there may be difficulty in arriving at common organizational goals and direction of effort. In a small general hospital, the surgeon, anesthesiologist, pathologist, and radiologist are individually powerful. If they elect not to agree on common directions for the hospital but, rather, to pursue their individual personal and professional interests, overall organizational goals, if stipulated at all, will be served only to the extent that the personal and professional goals of the medical staff are consistent with hospital goals. Under what conditions do coalitions form?

Consider the following organization of three individuals:

	Relative Power
Art	2
Bill	3
Carl	4

Each has power, and relatively, Carl has more power than Bill or Art, and Bill has more than Art. None, moreover, possesses enough power relative to the others to dominate choices in the group. The combined relative power of any two in coalition, however, is sufficient to control group choice if they so elect. Of course, the whole group could agree to act in concert or independently if they desired, but only two need agree in order to control organizational choice. Several questions arise from this simplified example. Which coalitions under what conditions are most likely? Is relative power a meaningful concept? What is the relevance of coalition formation in organizations?

Coalition Types

Mintzberg (1977) considers coalitions consisting of members *external* to the legal boundaries of the firm and *internal* coalitions. He notes three types of external coalitions, the types being dependent upon the degree to which their power is concentrated (Figure 3.1). Where a relatively large number of external pressures are brought to bear upon the internal system, the external coalition is passive in nature and unable to concentrate its individual powers to influence internal operations. Conversely, a dominated coalition can exert considerable internal influence to affect goals and behavior. A single majority stockholder/owner who wishes to exercise his ownership rights to direct the actions of the firm is an example. Sears Roebuck as the major customer of Whirlpool Corporation can act as a dominant external coalition, whose influence Whirlpool can ignore only at substantial risk.

A few external influences sharing power constitute a divided coalition, each member of which seeks to impose its own control over the affairs of the enterprise. A divided coalition is, according to Mintzberg, midway between a dominated and a passive external coalition in terms of the power it is able to exercise in goal formulation within a firm.

PROCESSES OF EXTERNAL COALITIONS

Table 3.1 classifies the types of activities undertaken by external coalitions to influence goal setting and behavior. The following review of activities used by external coalitions concerning foreign bribes by U. S. corporations is used as an example to define the several processes in Table 3.1 by which external coalitions influence an organization's goals and behavior. In the United States, it is considered unethical to bribe governmental, supply, or customer officials as a means of gaining favors. In some foreign countries, in contrast, such bribes are expected and constitute a normal way of doing business. To sell airplanes in some mideast countries, bribes to a relative of the ruler grease the way for settling final contracts. At one time, there was no specific prohibition against U. S. multi-nationals engaging in these payoff practices. The Securities and Exchange Commission has contended, however, that U. S. firms engaging in such practices must reveal the extent of their participation in them as part of the full disclosure requirement of their financial activities for the registration and sale of their securities. The social norms of United States business practice are thus, in effect, being extended to over-

Figure 3.1 Types of External Coalitions

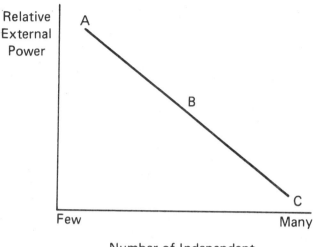

A = Dominated coalitions, concentrated power

B = Divided coalitions, divided powers

C = Passive coalitions, fragmented power

seas activity.   Although S.E.C. disclosure is not a specific constraint against such payoff behavior, it has much the same power as a prohibition.   Once such socially unacceptable behaviors are revealed, the public pressures to discontinue them become overpowering.

Aroused congressmen have, upon learning of overseas payoffs by American companies, introduced legislation to make such payoffs illegal.   Thus, the S.E.C. indirect constraint can become direct through new legislation.   As Table 3.1 shows, a more specific action by external coalitions is the pressure campaign.   Stockholder suits and stockholder associations were initiated in attempts to force company officials involved in foreign payoffs to repay such sums to the corporation, thereby safekeeping the financial rights, supposedly, of the stockholders.   In response, corporations asked auditing firms or blue ribbon panels of outsiders to investigate the extent of corporate involvement. Similarly, some other corporations established special investigating committees of their own board of directors (supplemented by outside investigative assistance, in some cases) to study and report upon corporate involvement in foreign bribes.

Table 3.1 External Coalition Influence Approaches

	External Influence Methods	*Examples*
Low	1. Social norms	Euthanasia is bad; speeding wastes energy.
	2. Specific constraint (or norm made official)	Euthanasia is illegal; trucks must obey 55 m.p.h. speed limit.
Specificity of Influence	3. Pressure campaign	Union strikes; boycotts by consumers.
	4. Direct access to decisions and the firm	Customer is asked to participate in cost reduction efforts.
High	5. Board of Directors membership	Banker participates in overall board decisions as member.

The cases of foreign bribes and payoffs illustrate all of the processes that external coalitions employ in their attempts at influencing the goals and activities internal to organizations. Societal norms formed the basis of criticism, specific constraints were applied, pressure campaigns mounted, and decisions by outsiders and board members were employed. It should be noted that as more directly influential external processes were beginning to be employed, the corporations involved began to appoint their own outside investigators and blue ribbon committees from the board of directors. In this way, it could be argued, these organizations coopted the processes that the external coalitions could have employed. It may be akin to an accused appointing his own jury.

INTERNAL COALITIONS:
THE CONDITIONS FOR FORMATION

In small organizations, a chief executive officer (CEO) may be able to establish organizational objectives and operating subgoals and practices by retaining control over the powers invested in him by the board of directors. Although the board supposedly has total power within legal and environmental constraints, the part-time nature of most director memberships means that the board cannot retain for a long period the powers that incorporation provides. Most of it must be delegated to the CEO in order for the system to operate. Although the board supposedly retains the power to select the chief executive, dividend policy, major resource allocations, and overall corporate strategy, Mace (1971) shows that the superior knowledge of the chief executive, in fact, allows him in many cases to obtain substantial influence over these board reserved functions.

By establishing a relatively small number of personnel systems, strategy and planning systems, and information systems, the CEO may be able to retain personal control to ensure that activity in the organization is directed toward the goals he selects. He can reward those who follow and punish those who do not. In larger enterprises, however, formal as well as personalized control and information means are needed. The groups of individuals designing and operating the resource allocation system in a larger firm, for example, establish a power base, since the CEO must rely upon their judgments in and detailed knowledge of the resource allocation process. In fact, top management may just be rubber stamping resource allocation choices made at lower levels (Bower 1972). Further, the goals of resource allocation can be subverted as lower-level managers manipulate their presentations of recommendations to satisfy their own interests rather than those established by top management and the systems designer. The mere size of organizations together with the differentiation of functions, then, tend to erode the potential power of the CEO by requiring delegation of powers to others. The sum of the parts does not equal the whole because of the inevitable errors in division into parts and the attention to them rather than the whole.

As an organization becomes systematized, bureaucratized, and tasks become differentiated, the imperfect matches that are inevitable between the subparts and the whole arise. Individuals seek to maximize the goals of their subparts, and suboptimization occurs. Even the measures used may imperfectly reflect the objective being sought. In the first chapter, the behavior and decision differences between using ROI and ROE as alternate ways of measuring profitability were discussed. Neither measure is completely adequate. Measures of subordinate goals suffer similarly. Suborganization interests and personal values of groups and individuals can be served instead of overall goals, if subordinates have the choice of measures to be employed. Thus, in the normal course of events in complex systems, the distribution of power and influence throughout the system by delegation is an ordinary result.

Expertise required in a system is a further incubator of potential coalition formation. Although most large-scale organizations are subject to attending to the demands of its experts, hospitals, commercial research organizations, and universities consist of a large number, perhaps a majority of the members in the enterprise. Because the primary impetus to the goals of such systems exist in the expert groups, the top management may be little able to exert effective power to weld the organization into a cohesive whole. In fact, Etzioni (1959) argues that the line management and staff roles are reversed in such expert-based systems. The medical staff in a hospital makes the important decisions, and the line administrative group merely provides the means for facilitating medical goals. Conversely, Mintzberg (1977) argues that the hospital board of directors, through its fund raising functions, derives substantial power over hospital goals and operations. Perhaps the prestige and status associated with board membership is sufficient to induce expected fund raising on the part of the board while expecting little power over internal operations in return.

VALUES, ATTITUDES AND INTERESTS

The origins and changes in societal and environmental values are important to assaying the power that external coalitions and individuals within the organization will exercise. The next chapter is devoted to a close examination of changing values and organizational responses, but it is important at this point to show how power combines with the values and attitudes of individuals to provide understanding of the content and level of objectives sought. Earlier in this chapter, the power of three individuals was presumed known. Consider the coupling of their relative power (from whatever source) to their commitment to a set of values. The example below simplifies this problem by considering only three values, but the principles it illustrates are useful.

Relative Power of Individual		Relative Strength of Value Held		
		Honesty	Efficiency	Stability
Art	2	6	5	3
Bill	3	7	5	2
Carl	4	2	4	8

Although neither Art nor Bill has as much relative power as Carl, considering their commitments to these three values, their attitudes are more similar to each other's than to Carl's. If either of them joined Carl in a dominant coalition, the values of honesty and efficiency would suffer in periods of no slack, since Carl, as the most powerful, would be concerned with stability. Thus, to explain who would join whom in a coalition of powerful individuals, an understanding of values held is useful. The goals of the coalition of Art and Bill would in probability include a consideration of, if not maximum attention to, honesty and efficiency. Stability might be considered if it did not interfere with the achievement of the other two, that is, if enough slack existed. It should be noted here that the science of measurements for relative power and commitment to values is immature; the numbers provided in this example are hypothetical rather than realistic for what can be measured. Furthermore, the example does not consider the potential bargaining behaviors that Carl could undertake. If he could convince either Art or Bill that long-run efficiency is most consistent with the stability of operations, he might be able to convince one of them to join him. It is also at this point that the use of side payments in various forms of policy commitments, in establishing inoperative goals, and in creating status positions could come into use (Cyert and March 1963).

Thus far, little has been explicitly discussed about the political activities that are directed toward personal goals or special interests rather than toward task performance and overall organizational goals. Even while carrying undesirable connotations, political activities can provide service to overall objectives. To illustrate, a group of foremen, dissatisfied with their treatment, pay, and status began an attempt to form a supervisory union in one company. This effort raised the question in the minds of top management as to the reason organizing activities were being undertaken. The underlying causes of dissatisfaction were identified and corrected, so that the bargaining effort and the reason for it disappeared.

Of course, much political action of organizational participants is directed toward the narrow goals of their subunit or toward their personal goals and interests. To the extent that political behaviors are widespread in an organization, the numerous goals pursued suggest actions inconsistent in total from overall goals. A politicized organization can create many small coalitions, none of which have sufficient power to dominate the affairs of the firm to lead it in a consistent direction.

THE ORGANIZATIONAL POLITICIAN

To understand how political activities in an organization can influence its functioning, the following paragraphs explore the means by which an individual can, through political behaviors, achieve personal and professional advantage (MacMillan 1978). A basic tactic is to acquire a key job or mission important to others in terms of information or decisions. If such knowledge or choice is needed by other managers, they become dependent upon him. The incumbent who must be consulted or approve choices thus occupies a powerful role. To illustrate, a large plant of a major corporation decided to create an industrial engineering department to eliminate bottlenecks in production and to install incentive plans for its operators. A number of bright young men were hired, and a large but relatively inexperienced group was assembled. The new department never contributed in the manner intended, because powerful established departments, such as personnel, operations, and accounting, were able to block, modify to their own interests, or delay any proposal made or implemented by industrial engineering. Although the industrial engineering department provided reasonable compensation and professional tasks for its own personnel, members questioned their contributions to the firm, because they recognized the political constraints under which they were laboring. High turnover of professional engineers was a result. The task was not recognized as providing centrally important expertise for the plant. Those moving to more influential departments were perceived as "smart." The power of review and approval in rival departments was influential enough to block effective action.

A second political tactic is to cultivate as social and professional associates those individuals with the status and position to aid the politician. Determining who can be helpful to one's career is important, of course, but making enemies of those of lesser importance often serves no immediate purpose and may haunt one later. Building alliances with peers, superiors, and subordinates is easier if these individuals can be made obligated to the politician. Providing impetus to the careers of "comers" in the system is an example of cementing personal contacts. But even if the relationship established is merely one of regular discussion or communication, this "right of access" can be important in receiving a favorable hearing later for projects and ideas important to the politician.

A third political tactic is to select those tasks to work on that have the highest probability of ultimate approval even if not technically superior. The manager of a major product line found that his close association with it killed his chances for promotion and viability in the corporation after a unique environmental discontinuity made the product obsolete. He was a martyr but not a winner. The complete politician develops the art of abandoning lost causes and associating himself to viable and popular ones.

Prerequisites to political success involve intensive and extensive knowledge of formal systems, informal systems, priorities, and people in the organization. Acquiring such knowledge is time consuming. Developing strong cooperative relationships with partners in coalition throughout the system constitutes hard work. It should be noted that this same knowledge and system of alliances can be just as useful in furthering the formal goals of an organization as they are to personal goals. Thus, adept politicians can be highly effective contributors to the organization, if they can avoid the stigmas of blatant power seeking or wasteful maneuvering. In fact, individuals technically brilliant may fail in fulfilling their potential if they are politically inept. Most ideas just don't sell themselves. Kotter (1977) contends that responsible adept political behavior is a key skill of successful managers. Although political behavior is often criticized as personally motivated and thus reprehensible, it can be directed as readily toward the benefit of the organization.

CLASSES OF INTERNAL COALITIONS

The conditions under which power is developed and used have been discussed. What kinds of internal coalitions result? In those situations in which the CEO is powerful, uses strategic control systems to enforce this power, and is able to dominate any formal bureaucratic systems to reinforce goal selection and achievement, the dominant coalition will consist of the chief executive. In some instances, a small number of line and staff personnel who share decision making and the design of those systems over which the CEO depends for his personal or formal control will share power with him. This kind of controlling dominant individual or group can be labeled as an *executive coalition*.

As the CEO delegates the development of plans and systems for operating the organization, new departments are created to design and administer them. As his detailed activities become numerous, the CEO can no longer keep track of what is occurring throughout the system. The subdepartments can operate independently of directions from the CEO. The CEO needs these subdepartments to carry on the expanded needs of his enterprise, but he tends to lose control over them.   At this point, the nature of goals and their formation can change.   If the conditions under which the organization operates involve considerable attention to subgoals, suboptimization of overall goals, and displacement of overall goals with subunit objectives or personal interests, the bureaucracy has taken over as the controlling force in the enterprise.   The dominant coalition has become *bureaucratic* in such a situation.

The *expert* coalition exists in organizations in which the professional goals of members override organizational goals.   In the extreme, profitability may consist of merely a constraint, enough profits being made to ensure survival.   The behavior of technical groups often results in the formation of expert coalitions.   A television manufacturer had detected the need for a moderate level of quality, intermediate priced products in the market.   High quality domestic producers were firmly entrenched in the market.   Cheaper sets were being imported.   A compromise between these extremes appeared to be a viable market niche for the firm to follow.   The chief engineer and the chief of quality control had their own ideas about the quality-price formula.   They had been concerned about the high reject rates and high levels of returns from distributors.   In redesigning the televisions to eliminate these problems, the quality level was substantially increased.   This level of quality also increased product costs, so that the original goals of seeking intermediate quality-price levels were displaced by the reject and return goals of an expert coalition.

The *political* coalition is one based upon the political activities of the members of the coalition rather than upon expertise, bureaucratic control or executive power.   Although powers in executive, bureaucratic, or expert coalitions may employ political tactics as well as other bases, a political coalition is developed primarily from political sources.   Widespread political activity throughout the organization may result in no coalition powerful enough to dominate its affairs.   Attention to goals, then, is to those goals the several coalitions set for themselves.   No perceivable overall organizational goals may exist if the organization is highly politicized.

COALITION OPERATIONS

Cyert and March (1963) developed the classical model of coalition formation and operation.   Their work is a basis for the following discussion.   The dominant coalition establishes the goals of the enterprise through *bargaining* among members.   As noted in chapter one, the Cyert and March observations of manufacturing firms identified five primary goals that were developed through the bargaining processes: sales, inventory, profitability, production, and market standing. These objectives and measures of them are not completely consistent with each other, so that all goals cannot be pursued simultaneously. For example, one production goal is to achieve long production runs, but this is inconsistent with a balanced inventory goal and the sales goal. To resolve inconsistency, the system pays sequential attention to goals by servicing first one and then, as powerful members associated with another goal insist, serving another end. Thus, although the production manager may be a powerful coalition member, he accedes to attending other goals to keep the system going.

The organization can, as long as it has a favorable exchange with its environment, continue sequential attention to goals since organizational slack, the excess of resources available over those required, is sufficient to satisfy the demands of all members in the coalition. In fact, the resource requirements to get some individuals to join the coalition may be relatively small. A policy "to produce the most technically advanced products" may be sufficient to convince the chief engineer to join the coalition. Yet this statement, if not made operational through greater precision and development of measures, is essentially nonoperational. It doesn't necessarily have any effect. Thus, at no real resource cost to the coalition, it has bargained for the talents and power of the chief engineer through a form of side payment, that is, a nonoperational policy.

Organizational learning takes place so that the performance of the system tends to improve over time. In addition, the performance of the system is affected by its aspiration levels relative to its goals. If performance exceeds goals, the aspired level of performance for the next period tends to rise to exceed past performance. If performance is substantially below the aspiration level, the goal is reduced to a point just above past performance levels. Typically, this process results in the creeping peg phenomenon, whereby the goal is slowly but continually moved upward as performance follows.

If external conditions of exchange with the environment become unfavorable to the system, slack is reduced. It then becomes impossible to meet all objectives. The goals sought by the least powerful members of the coalition are the first to be slighted. Under extreme pressures, only survival and profitability goals are attended to, a condition reminiscent of behavior in the classical economic model. Of course, that model assumes no slack can accumulate under the conditions of perfect competition. If a hospital suffers from lack of patients as it raises its prices to provide resources contributing to the prestige goals of its physicians, redirection of efforts occurs or the enterprise risks failure.

RATIONALITY OF COALITIONS

It should be noted that the degree of centralization of coalition power and the minimization of the number of its goals is related to the degree of optimization that a system can attain.   If a number of politicized coalitions persist in an organization, fragmentation of efforts toward the goals of the several coalitions is likely with no agreement of overall goals or attention to them.   In contrast, an executive coalition can agree upon a single or a few objectives, while possessing the power to direct all efforts of the system toward them.   A bureaucratic coalition is one that might be closer to the Cyert and March model, sequentially attending to different goals associated with the tasks and interests of the more powerful members of the coalition.

By attending to all goals some of the time, the bureaucratic coalition is partially rational.   The executive coalition is *approximately* rational as it focuses on a few integrated goals.   Fragmented political coalitions are *irrational* as related to overall organizational goals. An expert coalition could conceivably be any place along the rationality continuum but probably ranges most often between irrational and partially rational.   The concepts of rationality discussed in chapter one are thus seen as dependent upon goal setting and coalition operations.

ENVIRONMENTAL ADAPTATION
VS. SUBGOAL ACHIEVEMENT

Up to now, the reader may have gotten the impression that any number of expert, bureaucratic, or politicized coalitions can displace overall organizational goals.   Bureaucratic power stems from the organization's need for increased administrative expertise.   Expert coalitions stem from an organization's requirements for technical capabilities of many kinds.   Politicized coalitions stem from the skills of individuals to manipulate and negotiate to achieve goals they perceive as important, whether personal or organizational, in nature.

But how can such coalitions cope with competitive firms whose goals are more closely attuned to meeting environmental needs?   Resources come from the environment; they are not acquired internally. The whole concept of rational goal formation and strategy is based upon taking advantage of opportunities in the environment or avoiding threats while aligning internal systems to accommodate these tasks. Under what conditions can goal subversion, displacement, and suboptimization continue? We now turn to a partial answer to this question.

STRATEGY AND COALITIONS

In casual conversations about their companies, employees are likely to describe it in terms of the kinds of personnel or functions that dominate it. "We are a marketing company" or "our engineering expertise is the basis for our business," imply differences in the relative power of task groups within organizations as well as differences in what orientation the firm has with its customers. The purpose of this section is to provide a classification of coalitions, power, and goals based on strategic differences in organizations.

The central key expertise required in an advertising agency is often expressed as "creative talent" possessed by advertising executives and copywriters (or equivalents). One would hardly expect an accountant to become president of an advertising agency, since his analytical skills, even though substantial perhaps, are not those critical to the firm's well-being and growth. There are, however, certain firms more likely to have a former accountant as president. To show the conditions under which different coalition partnerships are formed, it is necessary to describe briefly the alternative strategies organizations can undertake. These categories are developed from the research of Miles and Snow (1978). It should be noted that these categories of strategy were developed initially from a study by Snow of textbook publishers. He found different internal structures and coping mechanisms in organizations facing the same environments. Yet other researchers, notably Woodward (1965) and Lawrence and Lorsch (1969) had posited that internal structure and process differences in organizations resulted from environmental changes and variations. The answer to this dilemma of where internal variations originate lies in the categories of strategy since confirmed by studies of electronic firms and hospitals. Both strategic stances *and* environmental variability influence internal structure and process.

DEFENDER

A company that selects a strategy focusing upon a high degree of efficiency in servicing a relatively narrow slice of a growing but stable market area attempts, often successfully, to become an important factor in that selected market segment. The defender company does not seek new products or services to introduce or new types of customers to serve, rather it attempts to gain through efficiency, cost reduction, and intensive attention to current customer classes an increased share of market. Thus, increased market penetration through customer and product service, as well as standardized design and price, characterizes their external orientation. Efficiency dominates the internal orientation. The internal efficiency is consistent with the external orientation and defense of its domain. The dominant coalition consists of production and financial/accounting executives, whose skills are most relevant to the efficiency goals.

PROSPECTOR

An enterprise that perceives its tasks as developing and selecting new products to service current and potential markets or customers is continually changing what it is doing and how it is doing it. As a prospector organization, its technology must be more flexible and adaptable to changing product requirements than that of the defender. At the same time, efficiency is less important than in the defender, since it must be able to meet a wide variety of needs rather than focus upon the narrow product lines typical of the defender. The prospector is, however, less vulnerable to major market shifts in product demands, since it has developed an ability to create, produce, and distribute changing services. As might be expected, the key skills dominant in a prospector vary from those of a defender. The prospector requires inventiveness in marketing and product development (for example, research and development). Not surprisingly, the dominant coalition in prospector firms consists of individuals from these functions. Its goals focus on *effectiveness* in meeting changing environmental and technological opportunities rather than upon efficiency in servicing a narrower market segment.

ANALYZER

Other organizations follow the strategy of basing a portion of their operations upon a relatively stable product/market segment and a second portion on adapting new products and entry into new markets. For the stable portion of their operations, the analyzer operates much like the defender. For the new product/market combinations that it decides to enter, the firm adapts the innovations developed by other firms. The analyzer must have a portion of its core technology stabilized to focus on efficiency and another separate portion flexible to service the changing requirements of the newly embraced opportunities. The skills required in the system include a means for identifying opportunities and their modification to the present system, while maintaining a basic core of efficiency within the stable portion of their operations. Accordingly, the dominant coalition in the analyzer firm consists of application engineers, marketing, and production. The goals of the analyzer focus upon both efficiency and effectiveness.

REACTORS

The strategies for all categories (defender, prospector, and analyzer) so far discussed are viable, workable, and a means for success (Miles and Snow, 1978). Each of the defender, prospector, and analyzer strategies provide a reasonably useful approach to the selection of products, markets served, technologies employed, and other aspects of strategic implementation (Hofer and Schendel, 1978). It is the consistent approach that is important in any of these strategies. Consistency does not *ensure* profitability or even viability, but inconsistency in their use is a prelude to disaster. The reactor category of firms found in the Miles and Snow research may have employed a defender strategy for one period, a prospector for another, and perhaps an analyzer approach at still another period. Since the technologies, product mix, personnel skills, and markets served for each of these strategies are different, the reactor firms were not, as a class, as successful as were the consistent strategies.

Whether the zigzag pattern of strategies in the reactor enterprises did not allow a long-term dominant coalition to surface, or whether the politicized nature of the coalitions in reactor firms prevented a consistent strategy is the chicken or egg question that is open to further research. The prospector strategy could be hypothesized to rest upon the impetus of an expert coalition; the defender upon an executive coalition; and the analyzer upon a bureaucratic coalition. It is too early, however, to speculate too far about these relationships or whether coalitions come before or after strategy. Alternative hypotheses are as reasonable. Additional longitudinal research is needed to help clarify such issues. It is clear, however, that reactor firms lack a coalition powerful and willing enough to establish a consistent set of goals and strategy for the organization.

The Miles and Snow research is relevant to our concerns in this chapter, in that it shows the patterns of coalition formation and operation are dependent upon the strategic orientation that the system takes vis-à-vis its environment. It is clear that each viable strategy is composed of a distinct differentiated group of dominant coalition members.   Politicized, bureaucratic, or expert coalitions do not emerge to dominate the organization, unless they are key to serving tasks consistent with the strategic stance of the system.

One further notion may be of interest.   The Miles and Snow measure of success or viability may not be consistent with the goals of the reactor firms studied.   If profit goals were ignored to emphasize the personal and professional goals of the participants in them, reactor enterprises may be considered successful in light of these internally developed goals.   In the light of what organizations are supposedly designed to accomplish for society as a whole, reactor firms were less successful.   Strategy and goal studies should, in the author's opinion, examine both internal and external objectives.

It is to some of the socially important external values and responsibilities of organizations that the next chapter now turns.

___

SUMMARY

This book is meant to help managers employ goals and goal processes in a manner more effective for their organizations.   A funny thing happens on the way to this ideal, however.   Political skill and power of individuals and groups can attempt to subvert the intended rational goal processes.   This chapter has been written to show how a manager can use his own power, skill, and coalitions to direct the organization toward intended results.   Furthermore, understanding how these political processes intervene allows the manager to fend off undesired actions.

In summary, we have shown:

1.   All individuals in an organization have some power even though small.

2.   Power comes from a number of sources:
—the ability to provide rewards to others
—the ability to punish others
—the desire of others to identify with a person
—an expertise in knowledge or skill useful to the organization
—because others think it is right for the person to exercise power

3.   Coalitions form from individuals with similar interests to exercise collective power.

4.   Coalitions form outside the organization in attempts to control its internal operations.
—the more concentrated external coalitions are, the more influence they can exercise

—the processes that external coalitions employ range from general, unspecific appeals to actual participation

A more detailed examination of external coalitions follows in the next chapter.

5. Size and dispersion of power in an organization give rise to powerful coalitions other than the chief executive.

6. Internal coalitions of four types may dominate the organization's goals and operations:

   —an executive coalition, consisting of the chief executive and whomever he selects to design and operate the information, planning, and control systems through which power is exercised

   —an expert coalition, consisting of a collection of individuals whose power stems from technical expertise

   —a bureaucratic coalition, a collection of individuals whose control over administration of systems within the organization provides their power

   —politicized coalitions whose power stems from political skill

7. Political skill and knowledge on the part of an individual can be developed, as can any other type.

8. Coalition power and political skill can be used to maximize overall organizational goals or to detract from them. Good managers develop political skills to a high level.

9. Attention by coalitions to organizational subgoals or to personal goals results in suboptimal performance for the organization as a whole. This condition and action is prevalent in large-scale organizations.

10. Several alternate strategies are associated with particular types of dominant coalitions:

Strategy	Dominant Coalition Members
Defender	Production, financial executives
Prospector	Product development, market research, research executives
Analyzer	Application engineers, marketing, and sometimes production executives
Reactor	No discernible pattern

11.   The reactor strategy is unsuccessful.   All the rest are viable and
      are related to a dominant coalition whose skills are consistent
      with the particular strategy.

   This chapter has laid the groundwork for a study of power and operation of coalitions.   It has also examined how goals can be influenced by internal coalition operations.   Within this framework, the
next chapter examines external coalitions as they form and develop
pressure on an organization to conform to values other than those
internally developed.

4

Environmental
and Societal Goals

The purpose of this chapter is to extend the concepts of power and coalition formation by examining external coalitions and other environmental forces from which external coalitions derive their strength. The major portion of the last chapter was internally oriented; this chapter is externally oriented. Together, the two chapters provide a picture of top management—attempting to establish rational goals and rational execution of them—being pushed from below to accommodate powerful internal groups and from outside to attend to environmental and social pressures.

It should be recognized that accommodating either internal or external demands alters the goal structure. Either more goals and constraints are attended to or some of the goals sought rationally may need to be lowered (or even eliminated), so that resources can be devoted to fulfilling new expected results. The chapter first examines organizations adapting to environments. An examination of social and environmental changes is followed by framing the analysis in terms of social responsibility. A final section then reframes corporate social responsibility in terms similar to those of the start of the discussion, namely, organizations as open systems adapting to their environments.

ORGANIZATIONS AS OPEN SYSTEMS

Hospitals, universities, business firms, and other organizations can better be understood if considered as systems continually interacting with their customers, suppliers, and the social, technological, legal, and political environments within which they operate. If the behavior of these external environments and institutions is stable, placid, and predictable, an organization can focus its operations upon maintaining that external stability while increasing internal efficiency. In fact, the firm following a defender strategy, as discussed in the last chapter, seeks out a market and product combination that is stable and large enough that its efficiency can be attained and maintained.

Variations in the environmental factors influential to the operation of the firm may be predictable (for example, seasonal sales variation) and taken into account. Consider the effect that seasonal sales have upon the system. Choices need to be made between the costs of carrying inventories, if a steady production rate is sought throughout the year, versus the costs of getting resources to meet production requirements during the peak sales months. Note that predicting the extent and timing of the external variation in sales is required if the system is to successfully adapt. The sales forecasting then needs to be coupled with cost and profit analyses of the impact of the two alternatives (varying production or inventories) as means for adapting. Additional organizational *differentiation* through adding the functions of forecasting and means of adapting is required. Then, organizational *integration* to couple these two functions is required as a result of the environmental variation. Galbraith (1978) provides an exhaustive analysis of differentiation of organization structures and processes together with the several means of integrating the resulting greater complexity of organizational functioning.

That some environments are more dynamic is illustrated by the differences in the technological changes in steel versus chemical firms. Steel firms expend slightly more than 1 percent of sales volume for research and development. Chemicals have a much more rapid rate of technological change to cope with, expending 3 to 5 percent of sales upon R and D. The relative size of product research and engineering groups in chemical firms is much greater than in steel firms. Strategy by selecting the kind of domains within which the firm operates can increase or reduce the amount of environmental variation with which the organization must deal. Prospector firms seek (and attempt to create) changes in the environment with which their flexible technology and skills can deal. Defenders seek to avoid uncertainty.

Just as market or technological changes create the need for internal adjustment, so do social, legal, and political changes. When the Joint Commission on Accrediting Hospitals seeks to implement increased safety from staph infections, individual hospitals may be required to alter their procedures, develop a task force organization to develop adequate procedures, and so on. Laws banning discrimination in employment have given rise to new positions in the personnel departments of universities, banks, and other firms.

Not all external changes are predictable. The Arab oil embargo was generally unexpected. Its impact upon auto, high use energy industries, homes, and the government itself has been substantial, and the whole country incurs costs in attempting to adapt to the changes implicit in OPEC functioning. Even defender organizations were not able to avoid the effects of the embargo. Because prospectors deal with market and technological uncertainties on a regular basis, one might expect them to deal with social or political changes better than defenders. Although not framing their analysis in the defender-prospector classifications, Bowman and Haire (1975) found high profitability to be associated with high social responsibility in foodprocessing firms. They hypothesized that both were effects from a high capacity for environmental adaptation.

HISTORICAL PERSPECTIVES

The political, legal, and economic environments within which U. S. firms operate have varied over the years. The U. S. political system was founded upon the principles of individual freedom and equality through democratic representative forms of political institutions. This freedom was extended to the means of production and distribution in the form of a free capitalistic enterprise system. At the beginning, laws and regulatory activities were directed at encouraging the development of manufactures and foreign trade. Encouragements were many and limitations were few. Mee (1963) contends that the ethical, religious, and social climate complemented legal and politician individualism. Economic and social progress flourished; the factory system displaced the craft systems predominant in colonial periods.

As markets expanded in the U. S. and as new technologies became available, large-scale enterprise came into being. Swift saw the potential in the refrigerated railroad car for concentrating slaughter, cutting, and distribution of meat to eliminate the inefficiencies of local butchering. Chandler (1977) shows that many inventive technologies were developed in the decade of the 1880s that allowed efficiency through large-scale enterprise. The pattern was repeated in shoe machinery, sewing machines, oil, tobacco, and other industries, but where technology did not develop (for example, dressmaking) to make large scale economically attractive, small-scale firms remain to this day.

The attractiveness of large-scale enterprise supported by markets sufficiently large to justify investments in the mass technologies led such firms to domination and control of markets and prices. Monopoly profits existed at the expense of most members of society, so that antitrust and antimonopoly laws were instituted to remedy perceived inequities. Similarly, the deleterious impact of employing child labor was recognized, and laws regulating such employment basically eliminated the practice. These events obviously changed the economic rules of the game under which organizations had been operating. From virtual complete freedom and encouragement to operate in whatever manner they saw fit, business activity was undergoing a change brought about by constraint and prohibition of certain behaviors.

In the more recent era, the managements of many firms perceive their environments as unfriendly rather than encouraging. The regulation of the issuance and sale of securities, the requirement to report profits by line of products, product warranty requirements, personnel hiring, promotion and dismissal rules and regulations, requirements to comply with the Occupational Safety and Health Act (OSHA), limits to information from executives during collective bargaining, pollution requirements, and so forth, combine to give the impression to managers that external environments influencing external operations are changing more rapidly and imposing more constraints. Executives question the viability of the free enterprise system under the burden of what many conceive as excessive regulation. Over the long term, institutions of most kinds have been increasingly constrained in the U. S. Since, as shown in chapter one, the difference between a goal and a constraint is more a matter of degree than of kind, organizations are required to allocate resources in order to achieve both goals and constraints.

Jacoby (1971) contends that the economic system is formulated, encouraged, and constrained by the political system. Changes in societal values are reflected more or less perfectly in the laws and regulations formed by political systems to control the behavior of the economic system.

Individual $\longrightarrow$ values held $\longrightarrow$ political system $\longrightarrow$ economic system.

As values of individuals are altered, they may influence the economic system directly, as exemplified by the response of American firms to demands from U. S. sources to correct inequities in wage payments to blacks in South Africa. In the case of air pollution, conversely, American automobile firms did little to reduce emissions until forced to do so by California and Federal legislation. Thus, Jacoby contends that it is the role of the political system to establish the conditions under which the economic system is to operate. The role of the economic system within the social and political environment is to supply the goods and services desired by society.

CHANGING SOCIAL VALUES

There have been important recent shifts in the values held by American society. Since these value changes are widespread and quite different from those held twenty years ago, their changing impact upon business and other kinds of organizations has not had time to be felt except weakly. Yet, these changes can have profound influence upon the goals sought by organizations together with their modes of operation.

The manifestation of these value changes was not evident until articulated by the student movements in the mid-1960s, although the students were merely coalescing value changes that had imperceptibly been occurring in the population as a whole (Yankelovich 1977). Additionally, the radicalization of the student movement stemmed from the Viet Nam War. When that war ended, radicalization stopped, but the value changes remained. Yankelovich's research indicates a diffusion of these values throughout the U. S. population, such that student values no longer vary a great deal from those of the general populace.

Yankelovich identifies the following recent transformations in values:

1. Hard Work.   Significantly less people believe that it pays off or is worth the 'nose to the grindstone' efforts to achieve success.

2. Authority and   There is a desire for release from constraints
   Restraint.   of: the boss, disagreement with laws, drug use, marriage role, family, religion, manners, morals, and patriotism.

3. Morality.   New attitudes and freedom toward sex, ration-
                       ale for war, kinds of friendships, interpersonal
                       relations, and attitudes toward property.

4. Self-fulfillment. A desire for self-gratification; less emphasis
                       upon sacrifice and role obligations.

5. Entitlement.   Individuals have basic rights to food, shelter,
                       health and education.

6. Naturalness.   Harmony with nature. Being at one with na-
                       ture versus strife.

Rather than to return to values previously held, Yankelovich sees
these as permanent, still-evolving attitudinal changes.

INFLUENCES OF VALUE CHANGES

The impact of these value changes has already been substantial.
These influences include the creation of substantial markets for
back-to-nature products (for example, diet, health products, camp-
ing), growing concern for the environment, proposals for universal
health care, guaranteed annual wage, antiwar demonstrations, sexual
freedom, acceptance of unmarrieds living together, women's libera-
tion, antidiscrimination regulations, and worker participation, to
name a few.

Lodge (1974, p. 64) shows some basic business implications consistent with and echoed by the Yankelovich findings. "Individual fulfill-
ment for most depends upon a place in a community, an identity with
the whole, a participation in an organic social process." This carries
the concept of individualism to a point that the person has a right to
self-fulfillment within a social (and organizational) context. Entitlement erodes the concept of private property upon which the corporate
form is based. The concept of competition is inconsistent with harmony in nature and the interdependence of all things. To control
the allocation of resources and services, the role of government
expands to replace competition. Finally, Lodge argues that spe-
cialization and fragmentation in the scientific areas is being replaced
by a need to look at whole systems not their parts.

At the level of legitimacy, these new values can have important effects. The legitimacy of advertising as a communicative and educational medium, for example, could come under attack for controlling
thought and restricting freedom. Whether profit maximization is a
goal consistent with these values could be argued. At the strategic

level, corporations are already entering or leaving businesses as a result of the effects of these value changes. One firm is attempting to divest its steelmaking business, "because the environmental demands are so great that reasonable future profits cannot be attained." At the operating levels, much work in job enlargement, participation, power dispersion, and other techniques have been initiated as means for coming to grips with these changing social values. From the questions of whether the corporation is a legitimate form to job design, these new values are important and need to be dealt with by managers.

Yankelovich (1977, pp. 63–64) argues that the 1950s were an era in which the social institutions were quite in tune with the desires of society's members: "hard work, economic growth, fertility, population growth, optimism, and accomplishment." Are those institutions that were geared to harmonize with the values of the 1950s inconsistent with the values of the 1970s? If institutions do not reflect the values of society of which they are a part, social cohesion and stability, in Durkheim's terms, are jeopardized. These value changes influence managers of all organizations in their ability to design and operate their institutions. Old solutions may not solve new problems. Universities, hospitals, voluntary organizations, business firms, and other organizations need to adapt to their external environments. The problem of the top managements of these systems is to identify the changes that are truly basic and relevant, whether organizational adaptation is desired, and the mode of adaptation most relevant.

EXTERNAL PRESSURES

Managements that respond willingly to every external and internal development lose the confidence of their clients and constituents. External pressures come from many sources, including groups representing splinter opinions. A country club board of directors that accommodates a few powerful members through its rules may alienate a much larger group upon whom the club depends.

Certainly the personal values of members of the dominant coalition can be imposed on the organization through the goals it seeks and the operating modes employed. In top management choices, in fact, leading textbooks advise that the values held by the executive coalition be transformed into strategic choices (Christensen, Berg, and Salter 1976; Christensen, Andrews, and Bower 1973). Without a consistent matchup of strategy and executive values, it is argued, strategic implementation will be jeopardized by actions contrary to strategy.

A difficulty of coordinating dominant coalition values with strategy, however, is the possibility that those values are not in harmony with the dominant values in society as a whole. Guth and Tagiuri (1965) show that businessmen score higher on economic values than do other social groups. But, of course, one would expect that. Similarly, directors of art museums might be expected to have high aesthetic values. The profile of values held by executives is important so far as the reflection of them in the organizations they lead is or is not consistent with a system well adapted to their value environment.

COLLECTIVE ACTIONS

Individuals with strong commitments to certain values and their implementation throughout society can usually find other individuals and groups expressing similar sentiments. Religious organizations promulgating moral precepts have existed since early history. The Sierra Club and Nader's Raiders are recent manifestations of groups formed to pursue the implementation of recently formed concerns. Whether these two examples represent mainstream or splinter group thinking is answered in part by the considerable resources that individual contributors have given to support their causes, together with the substantial effects they have had upon corporate operations. The Sierra Club was able to thwart a Disney-proposed California ski resort complex primarily by arguments that its construction would destroy forever an area of natural beauty and grandeur. Sierra's success in this instance is abetted by the increasing social agreement about valuing naturalness, as noted above in the discussion of the Yankelovich findings. This external pressure directly influenced the strategy of the Disney organization.

Local groups can be quickly and effectively formed to question, review, or oppose proposed highways, powerlines, and housing developments. Similarly, such groups have been initiated to bring into question long tenured practices of organizations. The point of interest to the managers is the recognition that such groups are probable and that individuals with common interests will form to achieve alterations in organizational performance consistent with the common values of their group. The effects of these external pressures are numerous: the need for managers to spend time to deal with the questions raised by the group; publicity, often unfavorable; frustration in completing new projects; the necessity of changing plans to accommodate pressures; delay and increased costs; nuisance; and diversion of efforts.

External pressure groups may be valuable to the organization by bringing relevant factors to the attention of the managers. At times, however, the interests of pressure groups may be selfish when considered from the point of view of the community or society as a whole. In attempting to meet the needs of its customers for electric power, a utility corporation initiated feasibility studies of a new line, identifying three potentially feasible routes. Each of these routes was opposed by the residents who would be most affected by land condemnation or visual interference. When the final routing was announced by the utility corporation, a group of citizens formed, hired a lawyer, and undertook to oppose the line construction. They questioned the need for increased power consumption above that served by existing facilities; they questioned the need for increased reliability by a route separate from enlarged existing routes; and they questioned the viability and supposedly lower costs of the particular route selected. The point of the example is the willingness and ability of a scattering of individuals with common values to form and develop an effective external coalition against an organization. The power line dispute was ultimately referred to the state utility commission for resolution.

GOVERNMENTAL PRESSURES

The utility example illustrates the use of a governmental commission to adjudicate disputes among organizations. Although final appeals to such a case may ultimately be decided in the courts, the impact of regulatory, legislative, and administrative governmental actions have substantial impact upon all kinds of organizations in both the private and public spheres. In theory, a democratic government reflects the values of the society it represents. As social values change, their furtherance through formal and informal nongovernmental groups provide impetus to the new concepts. As the impetus builds, individual legislators and administrators become champions of the ideas, propose legislative and administrative changes, and, if successful, introduce the embodiment of these concepts into regulation or legislation.

Advocacy and incorporating new values into the organizational environment is not a new process. Nor is the complaint by businessmen and others that governmental bureaucracies are strangling local discretion or free enterprise by their voluminous regulations and reporting requirements. What is more widespread recently, perhaps, is a more universal dismay from the governed of the perceived crushing magnitude of constraint and reporting in the U. S. system. City mayors decry the preparation costs of the huge justification requirements to apply for federal fund entitlements. Sewage systems, school supports, housing for the elderly, and similar programs have, in response to the desires of the electorate, been legislated with funds available to local constituencies who satisfy the program requirements. To ensure its will, the legislature creates a commission or assigns the task of administration of the legislation to some existing administrative body. The three Rs, reporting, rules, and regulations, emanating from the administration are one source of complaint of the benefiting municipalities. In similar ways, universities, business firms, symphonies, hospitals, and other institutions feel themselves enmeshed in a sea of paperwork and a noose of constraints.

PROFESSIONAL ORGANIZATIONS

The interests of individuals in disciplinary areas of knowledge or in the practicing professions underlie the rationale for the formation of professional and academic societies. The American Medical Association and the American Bar Association are interested in furthering the state of knowledge of their professions. In addition, the associations deal with issues bearing on individual practitioners and the whole profession as practiced throughout their domains. Insurance for malpractice has been an important recent agenda item for the national and local meetings of the American Medical Association. The influence of the association or local medical societies on the easy availability of medical care has impact upon state insurance commissions as they ponder malpractice rates for insurers.

Professional societies can have considerable impact upon the operations as well as the goals of ongoing organizations. AMA influences hospital operations, the bar association influences the courts and legal system, and the American Management Association influences how organizations are designed and operated. Although the output of professional organizations does not impose a great many constraints on organizations, the institutionalizing of professional practices can have considerable impact upon goal formation and achievement in an organization. If power is not concentrated in an executive or bureaucratic coalition (see chapter three), the opportunity for experts to subvert overall organization goals to serve instead the professional goals is present. In organizations whose personnel consist of many experts from different disciplines, the dependence of the CEO upon matching organizational activity to the professional inclinations of its most important resources may be substantial. Weakening central goals while strengthening independent professional goals can lead to goal displacement and power dispersion to the extent that unity of effort is unclear, if not dispersed. Professional organizations exemplify external organizations whose power to impose constraints upon other organizations exists and is exercised to some extent. Their more important impact, however, may be their member influences within organizations through introducing professional goals distinct from organizational goals.

EXTERNAL STAKEHOLDERS

In discussing external pressures upon organizations in the preceding paragraphs, the individuals, informal groups, professional associations, and governments have ordinarily no direct singular interest in the affairs of a particular organization. But for any enterprise, a number of distinct locally oriented groups have a direct continuing interest in the goals and operations of that particular system. The board of directors, stockholders, and employee unions are obvious examples of groups indigenous to a particular enterprise. The list of contributors to the fund drive for a hospital, the alumni of a university, and the members of a local political party are similarly directly concerned about the operation of a particular organization. The president of one university reflected the individuals and groups that commanded his attention when he observed that one-third of his time was devoted to operating the internal affairs; one-third to external, professional, and administrative concerns; and one-third to the external groups having direct stakes in the success of the system.

Customers grouped into associations can have substantial beneficial and constraining effects upon system functioning. A number of customers of IBM computers have assembled to exchange technical information, problems, and operating successes. Encouragement of IBM to provide certain software and operating systems designs has had a feedback effect to the corporation and its design-redesign functions. Apartment tenant associations have formed to solidify positions vis-à-vis landlords. The power of tenant associations is revealed by their collecting rents and withholding their payment to the landlord until association demands for services are met. The power of the individual tenant is extremely limited to withhold his rent, since the landlord can evict for nonpayment and refuse whatever service the tenant requests. If by collective action the tenants act in a similar way, however, the landlord's ability to redress his grievances in the legal and police systems is limited. In a thousand-apartment complex, existing individual families and possessions would encourage the political restraint of the police no matter who is "right" in the dispute.   This example illustrates group formation that has the effect of eroding property rights and enhancing entitlement and new morality values noted above in the outline of the Yankelovich study.

Specific attention to boards of directors and unions as external stakeholders in this section has not been given, but their interests and formation into coalitions with power to impose goal and operating constraints can be just as important as any other stakeholder.   The multiple constituencies of an enterprise and the multiple constraints they attempt to impose are not without countervailing influences within the organization that is the target of the external control.   It is to the organizational response and internal effects of external pressures that the following section turns.

ORGANIZATION RESPONSE
TO EXTERNAL DEMANDS

To understand how and why organizations respond to external pressures as they do, it is instructive to sketch a framework of the functioning of systems.   A number of citations could be given to clarify the sources of the research and hypothesizing about these effects. Thompson (1967), Galbraith (1978), and Richards (1978) provide the reader with points of departure, if extended study is desired. The following discussion is based on these and similar works.

The basic premise upon which the rationale for system response is based lies in the predisposition of an organization for stability.   An organization finds it efficient to provide stability to the operation of its technical core.   With stability, it can design its internal operations in the simplest, most cost efficient manner.   Extraneous activities can be lopped off so that a lean, streamlined system remains to service primary goal achievement.   The organization's members devoted to efficiency see danger in environmental changes that disrupt internal operations.   The external forces that, if permitted to intervene, would disorganize operations will be resisted.

The organization develops several mechanisms to ameliorate the influence of external variables and their uncertainty upon internal operations.   Buffering mechanisms that absorb the uncertainty influences before they affect technological core operations are a primary means.   As an example, inventory variations absorb product demand uncertainty so that the productive technology can operate at a steady, efficient rate.   Marketing modifies customer requests for special products by price advantages to produce decisions most preferred at the technical core.   Special products are discouraged through modular plugin components to provide customized products with standardized subsystems. A consulting firm specializes in certain standardized (for it) problems. A hospital refers extraordinary cases to others with capabilities that include the treatment of the malady as part of its technical core.

Planning employment and output levels provides another mechanism to accommodate perceived future uncertain events. Contingent plans provide alternative activity levels that are to be implemented, depending upon the environmental conditions the firm encounters during the planning period considered.

Irrespective of the modes of adaptation, absorption, or rejection of varying environmental influences, it is important to recognize that the system prefers certainty in the environment, rather than uncertainty, and that it undertakes absorption mechanisms to reduce being influenced by the changes occurring in the environment. The human body, similarly, can tolerate only a certain amount of environmental variation. The eye openings adjust to brightness and light glare. Body pores adjust to temperature variations to provide a stable internal temperature to the most important internal systems, especially the brain.

RESISTANCE AND STRATEGIC CHANGE

An initial response of the enterprise to external change is resistance or rejection of its validity or applicability to the organization. When it was first suggested that automobile exhaust pollution ought to be regulated, the auto companies countered that air pollution was primarily a result of industrial activity rather than motor vehicles. The industry rejected the contention that air pollution was significantly influenced by exhaust emissions. Considerable delay to ascertain the effects of motor vehicles upon pollution levels ensued, during which the technical core of auto production and distribution remained unaffected by the environmental pressure.

If it is not possible to avoid environmental impact on the technical core, management (or more properly, the dominant coalition) can divest itself of the system being adversely influenced to reinvest the divestiture proceeds in other activities. Strategic changes are drastic surgical relief from change influences. Textron was built through a series of acquisitions into a large textile firm, integrated from raw material to weaving, dyeing, cutting, and sale of customer products of the firm. As the viability of this integrated system came into question because of the variabilities of demand and supply at all stages of

manufacture and sale, the Textron response was to divest and reinvest in other kinds of businesses, rather than to attempt the long process of developing the internal systems necessary to successfully
adapt to the multiple uncertainties of the market conditions it faced.

RHETORICAL SUPPORT
AND TACTICAL DIVERSIONS

Although recognizing the probabilities of change, an enterprise may
wish to delay to provide time to work toward defeat of proposals it
sees as deleterious to its functioning. A professor and his departmental colleagues may give lip service to the new educational technologies of programmed instruction, self-study aides, television lectures,
and so on, while maintaining tried and true delivery systems in their
classrooms. Diversions can be investigated, such as exploring com-
puterized instruction as an alternative, before "throwing out the baby
with the bath." Although an organization may long protect its technological core in this manner, new organizations adapting to the
changed environmental conditions can emerge to supplant reticent
adaptors (Cooper and Schendel 1976).

ENVIRONMENTAL COOPTATION

Cyert and March (1963) contend that business firms negotiate their
competitive environments by industry standards and their common
practices through trade associations and other means. To the extent that competitor reactions can be anticipated in this manner,
market uncertainties are reduced. Similar approaches can be employed with other external groups. The strip mine operators in Illi-
nois joined the legislature in shaping strip mine regulations and legislation. By cooperating with external coalitions, the deleterious effects upon costs and competitive positions were minimized while undesirable social consequences of strip mining were reduced to more
tolerable levels. The success of this approach to reducing environmental uncertainties is revealed in the criticisms launched at regulatory commissions that they were the spokesmen or advocates of the
industry rather than the guardians for consumers of the products of
the regulated industry. The Federal Communications Commission has
been accused of fomenting the growth and profitability of radio and
television stations more than improving the quality of programming
efforts. The Atomic Energy Commission was charged with pro-
moting the use of atomic power plants while providing insufficient

safety in the design and location of plants. The implication is that the regulated industry was able to divert major agency attention to serving the needs of member enterprises rather than society as a whole. The potential external impact of the regulatory agency upon the industry had been coopted to directions originally unintended.

COMPLIANCE

Widespread voluntary compliance with laws is the basis upon which a democratic government is based. The Internal Revenue Service cannot check each individual and corporate income tax return to insure accuracy and lack of fraud. It must instead depend upon the goodwill of the populace to honestly report income and expenses. Similarly, a municipal sewage authority installs a tertiary treatment plant to remove prohibited stream pollutants incapable of removal by primary and secondary treatments. In a period prior to adoption of clean stream laws, a glass manufacturer designed and built a television tube facility whose effluent was "cleaner than the water purchased." The investment in this plant was ten percent higher than it would have been without the water purification equipment. Voluntary compliance with laws or design to avoid undesirable, unintended consequences forms the basis upon which a consonance of organizational actions with environmental pressures are accommodated. Rather than resisting the imposition of contraints from external sources, they are accepted. In voluntarily going beyond the existing pressures, an organization self imposes constraints which are attended to in much the same manner as any other goal of the organization.

PROACTION AND ADVOCACY

The tone of the discussion to this point has reflected the predisposition of organizational systems to seek stability and, therefore, to resist externally originated change. A more balanced and accurate picture of adaptation must also incorporate the leadership that many executives provide for enhancing social changes, both within their own organizations and others. The value profiles of managers in private, public, and voluntary organizations do not vary drastically from those of the public as a whole. Certainly, some managers embrace values as "liberal" as those of any other. If such managers are powerful members of the dominant coalition, the imposition of voluntary constraints incorporating these beliefs is more likely. Certainly, there have been a number of executives devoting their energies and organizational support to a variety of worthy causes as well as social movements.   The National Alliance of Business has been active in equal opportunity employment practices.   Individual executives lend active and, at times, strident advocacy to causes in which they have a strong commitment.

If an organization arrives at a strategy and set of goals consistent with executive values, it follows that many organizations will be quite consistent in their achievements with the general societal values expressed.   In fact, one would expect that in some enterprises there would be leaders in incorporating changing social values into their goals and operations.   While anecdotal evidence supports this position, data lending credence to it does not exist.   Considering that the most powerful individuals in an organization are those that have contributed to it for a long time, they are likely to be older and to hold the values socially dominant during their youth.   If so, there may be a likelihood of resistance rather than proaction to system changes from environmental variation.   Even if executives in dominant positions desire adaptation to external pressure, the inertia of the system through its buffering and uncertainty reduction mechanisms may inhibit the rapidity of adaptation that is desired.

SOCIAL RESPONSIBILITY

Closely connected to response to environmental change, particularly social change, is the concept of social responsibility.   Business firms are most frequently called upon to exercise a responsive stance to social problems.   Nader, however, is adamant toward government as well (Armstrong 1971).   The definitions of what constitutes a socially responsible organization vary from one extreme to another.   At the conservative end of the spectrum, Milton Friedman (1970) contends that the only responsibility of the business firm is to maximize its profits.   If this goal is not pursued singularly, society is said to lose its means of production and distribution, the prices of goods and services increase to consumers, and capital to produce future goods and services is lost if profits are not high enough to attract investments.   Leavitt (1958) echoes the costs of attending to social problems by the corporation, pointing out that executive actions to further a social goal sought by the executive constitutes use of stockholder rights in the wealth of the firm for unrelated purposes.

A neoclassical view of social responsibility (Burck 1973; Jacoby 1971) contends that the political system establishes the boundaries within which the economic system operates.   If society wishes business firms to provide day-care centers for children of working mothers, the costs of attending to these pressures increase product costs and consumer prices. In addition, if these costs are not incurred and the responsibilities are not the same throughout the world, the social costs incurred by affected firms will result in a disadvantage in selling in world markets.

A moderate position on corporate social responsibility contends that organizations have the power to negatively influence the social well-being (Davis 1975). The unintended dysfunctional consequences of economic behavior include safety problems with products, discrimination in hiring, and pollution. These social costs are the responsibility of their creator, since the firms have the power to create them.

The concept equates authority and responsibility as suggested in organization theory. Under this approach, however, it is difficult to understand why a bank has the social responsibility to provide low interest loans for college students. The banks have no direct authority over the spiraling costs of higher education nor the relative poverty of prospective students. Yet, equating power with responsibility constitutes the base for much justification of business activity in social responsibility.

Radical views of social responsibility contend that business enterprise should be in tune with the broad spectrum of its environment to such an extent that it recognizes and takes actions to ameliorate social problems. Business citizenship becomes the social savior under this approach. In a variation, Ralph Nader is interpreted as seeing the ideal system as the corporation "tightly controlled from above by the federal government" and "policed at the local level by what would amount to consumer soviets" (Armstrong 1971, p. 219). It is likely that such tight constrictions upon other institutions (for example, universities, hospitals, regulatory commissions, and so on) would be in order as well.

DEALING WITH SOCIAL ISSUES

These scenarios describe different conceptions of how responsible business firms should be. There is no right answer to how much a firm should engage in social responsibility. These decisions are choices for the dominant coalition to make, recognizing that attending to more responsibility has the effect of adding additional goal(s) or constraint(s) that use system resources. Recognizing that there is such a multiplicity of social causes to which an organization might respond, some observers (for example, Ackerman 1973) recommend that the organization's attention should focus on a limited number of issues because responding to everything will be ineffectual.

Ackerman recommends that organizations avoid responding to every social request put upon them. In terms of the criteria that might be employed to decide which social responsibilities an organization might respond to, Ackerman suggests that corporations, at least, focus on:

1. Issues that are of most *immediate interest* to the firm. Thus, a pharmaceutical company might address health care concerns; a computer firm could support rights of privacy issues; and a department store could deal with beautification and consumer problems.

2. Problems that have high *impact* or *value* to the enterprise. Thus, if water pollution standards are being established, it would behoove a paper company to participate in the debate about the standards because they will likely influence the costs and profitability of the firm.

3. Issues that, given the activities of the enterprise, will make a difference. Although it may be fashionable to support some currently popular social cause, the impact that an organization might have upon its success or failure could be minimal. The executives of an enterprise might find support for drug and alcohol abuse programs to be attractive. Although certainly these are important issues, whether the actions of a single firm can make any difference may be questionable.

4. Issues that are of local relevance. Since there is likely to be more direct impact upon an organization by the social issues in its operating locale, its focus upon issues of the immediate geographic area helps to ensure that the constraints it deals with externally are those of most immediate importance.

PROCESSES OF ADAPTATION

Given that an environmental social problem exists, the process of incorporating into a multi-divisional corporation an effective way of dealing with the issue is described in the research of Robert Ackerman (1973). In the first stage, the chief executive becomes concerned enough about the issue to formulate and issue an up-to-date policy about the matter. Because division heads are charged with the profit and cost responsibility rather than social responsibility, there is much lip service but little action to implement within the infrastructure.

At a second stage, the chief executive recognizes the lack of success and appoints a high-level staff officer to oversee company activities on the issue. Because of the staff officer's lack of authority to impose sanctions and because line officers are still rewarded for profit and cost performance, implementation in this stage also suffers. Yet the staff officer's work is important to defining the issues, gathering the statistics and analyses important to crystallizing the extent of the firm's involvement, and refining the official position.

At a third stage, the social pressures may have become more insistent, to the point that the chief executive feels the need to take a more direct hand in ensuring implementation. Overruling a subordinate or taking away authority of subordinates is a traumatic but dramatic demonstration of the seriousness with which the chief executive views the need for the organization to respond. Although this process may destroy the career of the overruled executive, it provides an example to the rest of the managers of the necessity to conform so that institutionalizing the adaptation can occur. Although executives view the processes as chaotic, Ackerman (1973) contends that these three stages have a logic that works and is useful. The period of time from recognition of the desirability of response to institutionalization took from six to eight years in Ackerman's sample. Recognizing these stages, however, could allow managers to speed up implementation.

CONCLUDING ANALYSES

The whole field of organizational adaptation to social problems and the embracing of some form of social responsibility is filled with discord. Advocates of one position or another can constitute harassment to the individual organization. Even dispassionate observers of the concepts of social responsibility differ from the views of Friedman (1970), recommending that business firms stick to maximizing profit, to George Steiner, suggesting that a whole new class of problems and decisions will become a normal part of managing in the future (Burck, 1973).

An instructive and balanced view of social responsibility is offered in the research of Bowman and Haire (1975). In their analysis to discover the relationship between the degree of social responsibility and business profitability, they discovered an inverted U-shaped curve. Up to a point, increased social responsibility was associated with higher profits, but further increases were associated with lower profit levels (see Figure 4.1). This result implies that firms engaging in widespread undifferentiated social responsibility activity also are the firms with lower profits. It suggests a need for focus upon the particular parts of social responsibility that have the most relevance to the firm. This is consistent with Ackerman's thesis, but the authors do not attribute cause and effect between profitability and social response. Rather, the analysis suggests that some organizations do a good job of monitoring and adapting to their environment, which results in higher profitability and moderate levels of response to social problems. Firms weak in adapting to their market and economic environments are both less profitable and undertake two separate social adaptation modes. Either they are unaware or they resist social response, or they attempt to do everything, little differentiating the important from the unimportant. This result also has implications for adaptive modes from resistance to advocacy.

Figure 4.1 Profits and Social Responsibility

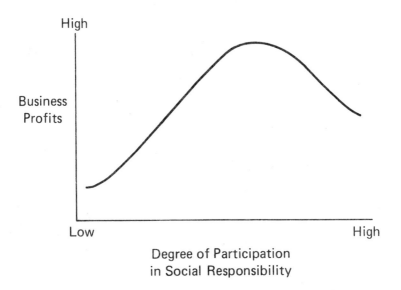

Finally, to those active promoters of social responsibility, it may be dismaying to learn that it takes six to eight years to successfully institutionalize a social policy in an organization (Ackerman 1973). In perspective, however, it also takes about eight years before a new product introduction becomes profitable (Biggadike 1976). Large-scale organizations are open systems adapting to their technological, social, and economic environments, to be sure. Whether this process is rapid or slow depends upon one's judgment of eight years.

SUMMARY

Rational goals and processes in an organization can be thwarted by both internal and external coalitions that impose different goals and additional constraints. These must be attended to much the same way that rationally derived goals are. In terms of external pressures and coalitions, the following can be summarized.

1. Organizations prefer stability to change, since their internal operations are designed to deal with a fixed set of conditions. Change, therefore, is expensive and resisted, ordinarily.

2. External pressures, if successful, however, induce adaptation of organizations to these pressures.

3. Major external pressures have their genesis in changes in values held by the populace. A number of major changes in values have recently occurred. These are being reflected in the heightened frequency and intensity of external pressures upon organizations. Organizations have not seen the end of pressures to articulate these changed values in organizational goals and operations.

4. An organization that seeks to continue operating on the basis of previously held outmoded values risks its legitimacy and effectiveness in society.

5. Corporate responses to environmental and social pressures include:

    A. Outright resistance.

    B. Rhetorical support, but no real behavioral or goal changes.

    C. Attempting to influence the environment toward goals sought by the organization.

    D. Compliance and internal change.

    E. Advocacy of social or environmental causes.

6. External social issues have become celebrated causes vis-à-vis the corporation. Models of how corporations should respond to social issues range from (a) the one extreme expressed by Friedman that a corporation's only social responsibility is to maximize profits to (b) Ralph Nader's position that corporations ought to be tightly controlled at the top by governmental action and from below by consumer monitoring activities.

7. Research shows that organizations that respond well in economic and technological terms to environmental change also re-

spond to social responsibility issues.   Such moderately responsible organizations deal with social issues

    A.   that are of immediate interest to the firm.

    B.   have a high value or impact on the system.

    C.   upon which the action of the organization can make a difference.

    D.   that are of local relevance.

8. By avoiding overresponse to social issues and yet by dealing with socially imposed constraints in a balanced adaptation, the organization can retain its economically based set of rational goals while remaining in tune with major social changes.

5

Goals and Formal Planning Systems

In competitively based economies there has been, during the last fifteen to twenty years, considerable corporate attention to formalized planning. Socialism depends heavily upon the state for developing and implementing formalized plans in the creation and distribution of economic output; private enterprise economies have depended upon the actions of individual business firms and the individual decisions of customers in free markets to determine the production, distribution, and prices of goods and services. In the light of this history, why has formalized planning suddenly become of such importance (Carson 1972) in the operations of business organizations?

WHY PLAN?

Two major reasons have been advanced to explain why formal planning systems are receiving the attention they have. First, as social organizations become larger and more diversified, their top management has a more difficult task of keeping track of what is going on within its systems. Secondly, if environmental uncertainties, as they bear upon internal operations, increase in frequency and degree of impact, top management may feel the necessity of establishing formalized systems to ensure that these variations are being properly attended to in the many subunits of organization. For example, policy

89

to achieve equal opportunity employment goals for minorities will likely be carried out poorly in some subunits of a large organization. Formalized corporate-wide plans to ensure meeting equal opportunity employment goals indicate at least partial compliance to objectives set with external coalitions of pressure groups and governmental agencies. The question arises whether the formalized planning efforts are effective and efficient in carrying out goal-directed activities.

Formal planning allows articulation of the intended purposes of an enterprise. As noted in chapter one, greater clarity of communication of objectives results in higher performance levels. The mere process of formalizing planning brings up questions about what goals the organization should achieve and what activities it should undertake in order best to accomplish them. Thus, formal planning requires an airing of views, an examination of the assumptions on which operations have been based and their validity, and analyses about the optimal means of achieving goals. Overall goals and planning systems can then be linked with the goals and plans of subordinate units. The whole process can clear the air, removing the mystique and secrecy of what is expected that often attend the aspirations and plans for the system when plans are in the mind of a single individual. Formal planning can provide openness, communication, and rationality, but does it work?

PLANNING PAYOFFS

A number of research studies have undertaken analyses to determine whether or not planning pays. Karger and Malik (1975 p. 60) comparing firms in three industries conclude that "top management of any profit seeking organization is delinquent or grossly negligent if they do not engage in" formal integrated long-range planning. Similarly, Ansoff et al. (1970) found significantly better subsequent performances for firms categorized as employing formalized systems and budgets to implement their acquisition activities. In general, these and other existing research studies heavily support the proposition that formalized planning pays. To illustrate the differences between formal and informal approaches, consider the alternative types of acquisition activities in the Ansoff study. Informal planners were opportunistic rather than goal oriented in the approaches used in acquiring other firms. Although they let it be known that they were in the market to obtain merger partners, they had no clear prior idea of which kinds of firms they sought. If a "good buy" opportunity arose, they acquired it. In contrast, the formalized and more successful organizations established specific goals, processes, and budgets for acquisitions. The criteria might include the industry in which to enter or expand activity, the size of firm sought, the relative position of the target firm in its markets, the past performance of the target firm, the quality of management, the adequacy of resources, the cost of acquisition, the willingness of present management to be acquired, and so forth. By establishing and employing such criteria to potential acquisition candidates, the formal planners were able to avoid "good buys" in dying industries with poor resources for future viability or in firms that did not "fit" the capabilities of the acquiring organization. Formal planners were more successful in achieving their goals.

RIGIDITIES VS. FLEXIBILITY

In spite of considerable evidence that formal planning systems are effective for specifying and achieving objectives, they are criticized for the potential bad effects they could have upon freedom and flexibility in an organization (Camillus 1973). One of the criticisms of socialist regimes stems from the inflexibilities introduced through formal planning from the top. If the U.S.S.R. shifts its overall priorities from industrial and military production to greater consumer output, the potential personnel and resource dislocations severely limit the extent such shifts in goals can be carried out. One large manufacturer in the U.S. established as a goal the achievement of a balance of approximately one-third of its business in each of military, industrial, and consumer markets. As it sought this objective, old priorities and policies required modification. To increase the consumer portion of its business, it acquired one business that needed an infusion of management and capital. As these resources were supplied from the other production divisions of the firm, the plans to achieve balanced goals reduced the capacity of the old divisions to maintain their former performance levels. Formal planning can thus introduce rigidities.

How should an organization balance its needs for certainty about how its internal operations are aligned toward goals through planning, while leaving the adaptiveness and freedom for innovation intact? McCaskey (1974) found that the design itself of the formal planning system constituted a means of achieving this balance. He found that one type of formal planning established goals, means, and controls in a logical, sequential arrangement. He contends that such a system is suited to mechanistic organizational tasks, relatively stable environments, and personnel seeking certainty in their jobs. Such a system focuses effort toward objectives, while providing tendencies for revisions and evolution rather than innovation and revolution. In contrast is the type of planning that only identifies the general domain in which the organization is going to respond and the actions preferred by members of the system to deal with this domain task. He contends such a decentralized system is consistent with an unstable environment, organic organizational forms, and staff personnel who seek variety and stimulation in their jobs. At the early embryonic stage of the product life cycle, a firm might employ formal planning of a less structured nature. When the same product reaches industry maturity, more structured and closer linked internal systems of plans toward goals become more appropriate.

The McCaskey dichotomy actually represents two points on a continuum from highly flexible to highly inflexible planning approaches. It is reminiscent of the Miles and Snow (1978) strategy categories of defender and prospector. All of the viable organization categories from the Miles and Snow research require planning. The content and, perhaps, the degree of specificity of planning varies. On the other hand, innovation and creativity are not inhibited. In the defender strategy, creativity is encouraged toward cost reduction and market penetration objectives. The prospector firm, conversely, invests creativity in new product forms. To contend that planning by a defender organization inhibits creativity is not completely accurate. The prospector strategy, in fact, inhibits creativity toward cost reduction goals, compared to a defender firm. Thus, planning does not inhibit innovation and creativity, but it does channel such behavior. Furthermore, the degree of specificity of plans and the closeness of linking planning to its implementation does have an impact upon the *kind* of creativity that is encouraged by the system.

ADAPTATION VS. INTEGRATION FUNCTIONS

Peter Lorange (1977) concludes that any formal planning system has two principal purposes for an organization. The first one serves as the link between the organization and its environment, ensuring that the firm's outputs and its activities are consistent with the external milieu in which the enterprise operates. This is the entrepreneurial task of *adaptation*. A formalized procedure for scanning the state of technology, competitors, customer needs, and sociopolitical trends would supposedly constitute one component of the adaptive response mechanisms of a formal planning system. The development of synthetic wash-and-wear fabrics brought about the need to redesign laundry equipment to clean clothing made from these new fabrics.

The laundry equipment manufacturer who first perceived this change in clothing and adapted the wash cycles on its laundry equipment products placed itself in a competitively advantageous position for a time. Whether such a change was best perceived by formal or informal means in this particular instance is an open question. Yet the overall need for viability of adaptation functions in planning systems appears solidly based.

STRATEGIC MONITORING

In a multi-product firm producing laundry equipment, television sets, and other consumer durables, the change to synthetic fabrics has no impact upon television production or sale. Further, since the corporate offices may be concerned with many different products and markets, can the corporate level monitor changes better than the product division responsible for the particular product/technology/market? Some firms resolve this issue by corporate-level planning, insisting that product divisions maintain research or engineering sections to stay on top of or to create new technologies applicable to the division's product domains. The role of corporate policy is first to ensure that this divisional monitoring is accomplished. But there may be new technologies emerging to provide completely new products capable of providing the same services that current products provide. Corporate and divisional planning systems could be engaged in the planning to deal with such threatening developments. Similarly handled may be the developing technologies that hold promise of providing new products relevant to the strategy of an organization. The developments in tape recording technology are important to the ability of a consumer durable manufacturer to design and manufacture a home video tape recorder. Although the firm may have no such existing product, the potential for goal relevant new products in technologies distant from those used in existing products suggests the need for the formal planning system to provide the monitoring of such environmental changes. To fully achieve the adaptation function, the formal planning system needs to incorporate scanning activities, not only for technology as noted above, but also for sociopolitical trends and economic and competitor activities.

INTEGRATION PLANNING

Lorange's (1977) second purpose for a planning system is that of *integration*, through which the organization helps to ensure that those

activities necessary for establishing and achieving goals are undertaken in a coordinated manner. A formal planning group that develops an overall strategy "to provide high quality, large-volume equipment, and appliances for home use" still has the task of determining
whether to produce and sell a home video recorder. Several U.S.
firms have decided not to manufacture video recorders but to pur-
chase for resale already designed products from Japanese manufacturers. If, however, our hypothetical consumer durable enterprise
chooses to manufacture, additional plans to assemble and deploy resources are also required. The selection of strategy, products, and
target markets to meet business goals is not enough. In planning societies, there is the suggestion that a number of *key management systems* need to be developed and integrated with product/market strategy to insure goal accomplishment. What are these systems? The
major suggestions are discussed in the following paragraphs. Table
5.1 presents a preview of how illustrative systems contribute to business goals.

RESOURCE ALLOCATION SYSTEMS

Providing physical and working capital needs consistent with strategic choices is an ongoing organizational problem. In a multi-product
system, a particular capital request from a cash cow business may
show high cash returns and a short payoff period. Conversely, a
growing high potential star may only show long payoffs for its needs.
In fact, the models and criteria most commonly used for capital allocation may favor old products rather than new ventures. Because
of the uncertainties in new undertakings, the financial returns of
such proposals may be discounted to such an extent that they appear
less profitable than investments in existing products. Models using
cash flows aggravate this bias. Redesign of such systems to provide
a goal balance between (1) growth and renewal of existing products
and (2) initiating new projects appears needed. The arbitrary allocation of a portion of total available investment funds for new ventures in any one year is one method—probably a very suboptimal one
that does not provide balance between specific projects (but might
provide overall corporate balance to strategy).

A model that theoretically could achieve the optimal allocation of
available resources among competing projects is "net present value,"
which allows one to equate all future returns and costs from different
projects to overall financial objectives. This method still suffers
from the relatively high discounting of uncertainty in the estimates
of the value for new projects. It does eliminate the biases existing in

payoff models, the most commonly used decision model for resource allocation in the U.S.

POLITICAL CONSIDERATIONS

Bower (1972) provides insight into adjustments made in estimates for requests of capital by lower-level managers. By changing projected sales estimates or margins, the "right" revenues can be shown to justify the capital requests *if* managers at higher approval levels are convinced that the project warrants encouragement. Thus, if strategy is approved, investment requests can be made to justify the strategic choice. In this study, new investment projects (and inherently, strategy choices) were initiated at lower organization levels rather than at the top. Part of the reason for this seemingly politicized approach to new products and investment in a multi-product firm may stem from the lack of linkage of the resource allocation objective with business planning goals in the corporation studied.

The reason for discussing resource allocation as one of the key systems for achieving integration in formal planning systems is to show its link to achievement of goals. If resource allocation is not coordinated with other strategic plans, managers will find themselves in the position of one manager described by Bower (1972). He was encouraged by approval of a large investment request to initiate mass production of FIREGUARD, a new product. On the other hand, he was asked through his business planning reviews to improve the profitability of his total activity, but FIREGUARD was increasingly unprofitable. The manager, rather than the planning system, was asked to reconcile these conflicting pressures between the current profit and growth goals. The development of a total strategic planning and management system consisting of a subsystems key to formulation and achievement of strategy would, ideally, link resource allocation processes to the other planning systems. Such goal conflict would, then, be minimized.

FINANCIAL PLANNING AND BUDGETING

Formal planning in some organizations consists wholly of rather short-range financial planning. At the simplest end of the spectrum, these may be based on extrapolation and summation of functional plans that generate revenues and incur costs. As discussed in chapter one, overemphasis upon short-run financial performance runs the

Table 5.1 Relations Among Planning Systems and Business Goals

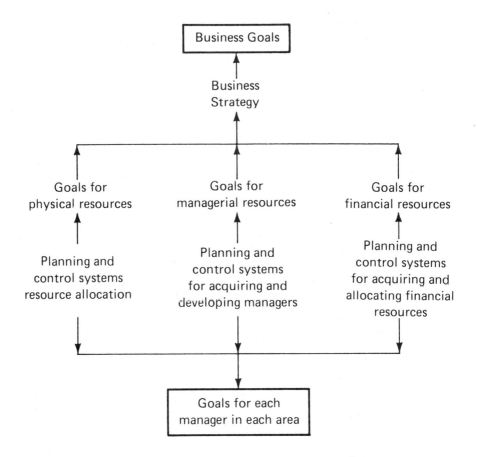

risks of suboptimization of performance in the longer run (Drucker 1954). To reduce such risks, modern organizations not only establish multiple goals but also several independent, but linked, systems to ensure achievement of other than financial goals. Yet, the yearly budget planning and the reviews of actual financial performance against such planned activity constitute an integral part of any formal planning and control system. Financial returns are, after all, the bottom line.

With respect to strategic management, an important issue to be dealt with for financial planning and budgeting systems is the degree of linkage desired across systems. This issue was illustrated by the example of the FIREGUARD manager above (Bower, 1972), whose entrepreneurial objectives were interfering with his achieving financial goals. In a firm employing a five-year financial plan and a yearly budget, the first year of the financial plan should be closely consistent with the yearly budget if tight linkages are sought. If there is no formalized relation between the two, managers will merely be going through "corporate exercises" for the system, which is not given attention. Considering the common pitfalls in planning, one would expect overemphasis upon short-run activity, that is, budgeting, to the detriment of the five-year plans (Steiner and Schoolhammer, 1975).

MANAGERIAL RESOURCES

Needs and Development

Systems for the acquisition and development of managerial resources can be as important to goal achievement as physical or financial resource systems. Comparing two businesses, one with a sustained 15 percent rate of growth in revenues and one with a 5 percent rate, the former will double in size in about five years, and the latter will require over fourteen years. In slow growth situations, a firm may be able to rely upon the natural development of existing managers to supply future managerial resources. Even at stable activity levels, however, an organization may suddenly find itself critically short of managerial talent if the top executive cadre retires or resigns within a short period. To avoid unpleasant surprises of this nature, plans to accommodate executive turnover rates and the expected creation or elimination of managerial positions because of changes in activity levels can be established.

Organizational Planning

Organizational planning to alter structural arrangements is related to present and planned objectives and strategic positions of the enterprise. As the greater relative emphasis in attention to research was established as a goal of a university, the president asked his staff to determine whether auxiliary assistance should be created to facilitate faculty preparation of research funding proposals. Further, he sought answers to whether, if established, the facilitation offices should be created at (1) the departmental, college, or university levels, or (2) at multiple levels. The strategic change generated a potential need for changes in organization structure. For corporations, structural changes are severe as the firm moves from an entrepreneurial stage to a professionally managed single product stage and, then again, when diversity in product line characterizes the strategy (Galbraith 1978). An organizational planning system is used to develop future needs for managerial resources.

As part of such a system, a review is made of the degree that managers are backstopped by potentially qualified replacements. If the potential replacements possess severe weaknesses for stepping into vacated advanced positions, their personal development toward the needed managerial expertise can be undertaken. To identify strengths and weaknesses of individuals for performance in present and advanced positions, some type of performance evaluation for managerial personnel is required. The next chapter examines Management by Objectives (MBO) systems as they can contribute to this development and evaluation goal.

Recruiting

In a given organization, it turns out that the managerial ranks are replenished from many interior and, in many firms, exterior sources. Certain kinds of nonmanagerial positions, however, tend to contribute more heavily to managerial positions than others. In organizations following defender strategies, for example, one would expect the production and finance functions to contribute the bulk of managerial members to the dominant coalition. As the organization identifies the major internal sources for its first-level managers and the alternate patterns for this advancement, the establishment of key nonmanagerial positions to which individuals with high potential for responsibility in management can be made. Since managerial personnel are increasingly those with advanced education, college recruiting goals often focus some attention on obtaining graduates to fill entry-level but key nonmanagerial positions. As individuals undertake these roles, their suitability for moving into management can be assessed.

Compensation

A final aspect of obtaining and using managerial resources involves the compensation system used for management personnel. The motivation of managers is dependent to a great extent on the manner in which compensation rewards are related to managerial performance. As noted in the last chapter, product division managers paid lip service to achieving corporate social responsibility objectives, while directing their ongoing activity and resources to profit achievement, on which their monetary incentive compensations were based (Ackerman 1973). It was not until their jobs or their compensation systems were jeopardized by intervention of the chief executive that institutionalization of the desired social objectives was achieved. Similarly, if the strategy calls for new products, the shakedown of new facilities, the widespread development and schooling of personnel or other activities that have the tendency to detract from short-run financial results, any incentive compensation schemes based upon achieving specified profit levels will misdirect attention away from a balanced set of multiple objectives. The compensation system needs to be designed to reward managerial performances in the multiple areas established as goals for the particular manager's job. It is the link between expected organizational performance and the manager's personal objectives. Proper rewards also ought to be linked to achievement of the several goals for which the particular manager is responsible. Since the objectives that the field sales manager should meet are considerably different than, but related to, those that the advertising manager should achieve, the evaluation and pay of each, ideally, should be individualized to reflect how well predetermined goals have been met. Organizational goal displacement to personal or subunit objectives can be minimized if compensation is tied to desired results.

Summary

To summarize about the planning that contributes toward ensuring managerial resources, it is evident that a number of interrelated subsystems are involved, including systems to project managerial vacancies; to recruit seasoned executives from outside the firm; to evaluate performance within the firm for counsel, pay, and potential promotion; to pay executives in relation to how well they achieve multiple goals; to help backstop key executive positions with replacements; and so forth. These results are shown in Table 5.2.

The goals sought for managerial resources should ideally be related to strategic business objectives. The director of management development for one large multi-industry firm established a ratio of 1.0 backup or potential replacement for each of the firm's top 200 executives. This implies at the extreme that there should be twice as many qualified individuals as there are positions. This may be realistic if executive turnover and corporate growth are high. The ratio could be considerably less for a stable firm with low managerial turnover. In fact, too high a goal for backup personnel may increase

Table 5.2 Planning Systems and Goals

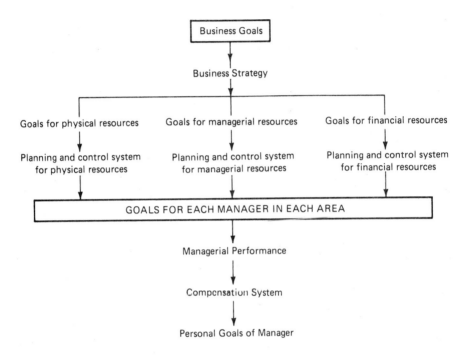

NOTE: Not all goals nor all planning systems are shown.

managerial turnover, as qualified executives tend to leave to seek increased responsibilities in other organizations. The key point is that the goals of the planning for managerial resources need to be linked to other key planning systems and their goals, in order that the integration function of formal planning is served.

MANAGERIAL CONTROL

Establishing a set of plans coordinated with strategic goals provides the direction and expected level of activity the organization is to follow. Control is a process of monitoring and evaluating actual performance as progress is achieved toward those goals. The monitoring process involves an information system that records, summarizes, and provides comparisons of actual to planned goal measures. Some writers, therefore, contend that the control and management information systems constitute key subsystems in an integrated planning system oriented toward the integration function.

PLANNING SYSTEM PURPOSES

As shown above, a number of subsystems are relevant to the purposes of adaptation and integration. How well do planning systems deal with these two ends? It is clear that the integration task for implementing strategy through formal planning systems is achieved with greater regularity and success than is the adaptation purpose (Lorange 1977). In fact, some would question whether or not the creativity and innovation required in adaptation can be achieved through formal means. Groups do not create ideas, individuals do. Examples of visionary master strategies suggest the central role of a creative individual rather than the result of formalized planning procedures. Strategic change and even major changes in integration modes in organizations appear to be related to changes in chief executives. At least, considerable skepticism surrounds the question whether adaptation can be achieved successfully by a formal planning system.

Can formal planning play *any* role in adaptation? Yes. Systems of scanning the environment, analysis of external trends, and analysis of proposed strategic moves probably constitute major adaptive roles to which formal planning can attend. As these data are reviewed by the strategist, whomever may be involved, at least intelligent inputs on which to attempt to develop further the strategic position of the organization are available. In addition, research and development and external acquisition departments are sources of potential adaptive activities in which an organization might engage. These groups may not create strategy, but they can develop potential entrepreneurial activities for strategic choice. It should be noted that encouraging one line of business and discouraging others constitutes a change in adaptive emphasis. The planning system ought to be able to identify one of its businesses as a dog if it possesses low market share in a slow growth industry. At that point, resources can be withheld from it or attempts made to sell the line of business, an adaptive action.

Adaptation of the enterprise in the external sociopolitical realm does not necessarily involve new ventures on the part of an enterprise. As part of formal planning, a suborganization devoted to monitoring these developments may provide a useful function for the chief executive and the organization as a whole in its attempts to respond to social and environmental pressures.

Looking closely at the activities in which formal planning might service the adaptive purpose suggested by Lorange (1977), it is evident that there are many of these activities. However, most are peripheral to, not a central core of, adaptive decisions.

TIME SPANS IN PLANNING

Some formal plans are *periodic*, including budgets, five-year plans, quarterly reviews, and so on. Others are *standing* plans that are continuously in effect until altered. Reviews and alterations of standing plans are not necessarily periodic but occur as needed. Standing plans include corporate strategy, business strategies, policies, and some procedures. Still other plans such as projects and programs may be limited in duration, but their ending point is indefinite: military hardware contracts, shipbuilding programs, and so on. At any particular point in time, an organization may have any and all of these classifications operating alongside one another. The managerial problem is to ensure that each is initiated and reviewed in consonance with their differential periodicity and importance. Only in such concordance can they work as intended to achieve goals.

Since the structures of plan hierarchies were discussed in chapter two, it is not necessary to review those patterns here, except to emphasize that top management and the planning staffs assisting the top line executives ought to be constantly aware of the need to ensure that goals of subunits are directed toward achieving goals at higher levels. To reduce, through planning, the amount of suboptimization arising out of attention to subgoals is not an easy task.

Time Phasing

In a product division of a large aerospace firm, the general manager noted that he had 200 separate projects under contract at one time. Each had separate starting dates. Some had specific termination dates; others did not. Each was in a different stage of completion. Each required a different amount of resources of the division from personnel, engineering, tooling, testing, production, and quality control. The requirements for design work upon the engineering department, for example, could vary from week to week as different projects were completed, delayed, or started. New projects were sought to minimize fluctuations, but more important in seeking new business was divisional profitability goals and the division's strategy. Corporate-level planning constrained the charter of strategy for the division, so that only tasks that best met divisional capabilities were to be sought. Other potential tasks were chartered as the strategic domain of other divisions of the firm. The relative expertise of the several divisions warranted the different division strategies. Nonetheless, the division manager's planning task was a complicated one, trying to phase projects to functional plans to overall divisional plans to corporate-level expectations of the division. Evaluation of functional managers was difficult, because the performance of the engineering department, to pick one, depended upon how well it had performed on each of the projects it had worked on during the period involved. Similarly, it was difficult to plan and evaluate the performance of program managers in charge of projects, because their performance was dependent upon the performance of the functional departments whose resources their project employed. The division manager considered integration of across-time and among-hierarchical levels one of his most important planning tasks.

One might contend that the multiple plans in this situation are additive, so that integration merely involves:

1. Bidding for contracts that correspond to the division's charter of strategy from the corporation.

2. For successful bids, schedule the project to meet its delivery requirements. Develop the required functional inputs and the sequence of time periods that these inputs must be undertaken in order to meet contract deliveries.

3. For any period, say a week, any function will be able to determine its workload by summarizing from project schedules. Adding any nonproject time provides the total workload for the functional week and, from that, the number of personnel and their assignments. The workload can, if need be, be costed.

4. A quarterly or yearly budget of costs by functional department can be established by summing weekly workload costs.

5. Revenue projections by time period can be made by summarizing the payment schedules in the project contracts.

6. Estimates of overhead and other costs can be made from activity levels and past period costs.

7. Profit, return on divisional investment, cash position at any time, inventories, and so forth, can be projected from starting positions and activities noted in 4, 5, and 6, above.

8. The results can then be used to bid on future contracts more likely to achieve divisional profitability, growth, and developmental goals.

This sequence is straightforward, logical and, to a certain extent, lower-level goals are integrated with divisional and corporate-level objectives. The scenario, however, ignores some undesirable effects and many uncertainties. First, some functions likely will be overloaded as many projects seek their capacities at the same time. Project scheduling must be coordinated and negotiated with each function.   The most politically skilled project manager may be able to obtain schedules from all needed functions, while other project managers have delays.   Project priorities need to be established at higher levels (for example, the general manager) to schedule them in such a way as to best contribute to divisional goals.   Design changes and unrealistic estimates invalidate prior plans.   This requires adjustments in schedules, costs, manpower plans, and others.   A host of other problems and uncertainties can arise to complicate the planning and control systems within a division's total planning.   The simple additive model is unrealistically simple if these other factors are considered in planning.

Levels vs. Time Span

It should be noted that there is a rough correlation between the length of the planning period and the level of hierarchy involved in developing and using the plan.   Top management carries the responsibility of looking out for the long-term influences on the system.   Lower-level managers may be working upon plans for a month or a week.   Although top management may appear to be involved in many day-to-day activities (Mintzberg, 1973), their longer-term planning responsibilities are equal to those involving current operations.

PLANNING PROCESSES

A question that planning theorists wrestle with is whether planning should be from the top down or bottom up.   When a complete top down approach is used, top management or its planning staff establishes overall corporate goals, designs the master strategy to guide acquisition or divestiture of businesses, develops the goals and business strategy for each separate business unit in light of such factors as its position in the growth-share matrix, and is active in formulating the functional plans for functional departments within a business unit.   One implication of this type of planning is that the dominant power coalition is an executive one with the influence to gather the requisite data about relatively low-level activities, so that they can be employed in the planning process.   The advantage of such a system is that the important plans can be made to rationally interlock in a hierarchical and time phased sense with overall objectives.

One class of firms in which the executive coalition dominates consists of entrepreneur-managed firms. Because the creator of the business, the entrepreneur, views it as his mistress (Collins and Moore, 1970), he brooks no sharing of authority with other managers. He seeks to know about all phases of the business and may freely interfere with decisions made by his subordinates. Whether formal planning can be said to exist in such an organization is an open question, since the owner can reverse his own or others' prior decisions with propriety.

In contrast, consider an organization with highly politicized dispersed power coalitions, each of which has insufficient influence to dominate the planning decisions of the organization, be it a business or other kind of enterprise. Although each coalition may be able to determine how the part of the total system it influences shall operate, the overall plan, if any, would merely consist of a summation of these individual parts. Although a planning group at the top could fashion a comprehensive plan, its impact would be slight since the power to enforce it would be absent. In this extreme, bottom-up planning is an accomplished fact.

Between the extremes of the entrepreneur and the politicized groups are the more realistic and frequent cases of combined bottom-up and top-down planning processes. As an organization grows to encompass a number of lines of products and a divisionalized structure, the executive coalition finds it impossible to acquire enough information about what is going on to plan and control in an adequate manner. Bottom-level knowledge is needed to build realistic plans. This requires top management to accommodate the expertise in the subunits and to share power with them. At this point, the bureaucratic coalition can exercise its powers to establish plans favorable to the subunit but contrary to overall goals. Suboptimization has then set in. Of course, the personnel in one subdepartment often are unconcerned about the negative effect of maximizing subgoal achievement upon overall goals or upon activities in other departments. This is no more evident than in the defense department budget process, where the Army fights the Navy, and both fight the Air Force. It was the contribution of Robert McNamara as secretary of defense to establish the overall missions and goals to be performed by the armed services. Then the expenditures allocated to one arm of the service were based upon its relative contribution, determined through cost/benefit to preplanned missions. Interestingly, one method McNamara used to consolidate power was to create a huge bureaucratic coalition at the top level, while limiting staffs at each service secretary level. At one time, the defense department had 7,000 people at its headquarters, and the secretary of the air force had 300.

PLANNING CYCLES

Because there are joint efforts at different levels and because efforts at each level are dependent upon plans completed at other levels, all of these planning processes cannot be undertaken at the same time. This condition leads to a sequence of planning steps that is initiated at the top levels and triggers lower-level planning that then is returned to be reviewed at the top level. It is cyclic in the sense that the process steps end where they started—at the chief executive's office. Lorange (1977) specifies the steps in setting objectives for the multi-product corporation as a whole as:

1. The CEO states corporate objectives.
2. The CEO calls for divisional plans.
3. Each division head defines his division's charter and its business rationale.
4. Each division head proposes division goals and resource requirements.
5. The CEO approves division objectives and strategy.
6. The CEO states corporate strategy and tentative corporate and divisional goals.

The process takes advantage of the expertise at each level. The division heads know their individual businesses well and are able to position them in their environment in the most advantageous manner. The process requires them to give consideration to the important aspects of planning, that is, their goals and divisional strategies. The chief executive can establish corporate goals in the light of what the subunits state they can achieve. Further, the data on divisional strategies, goals, and performance allows the CEO to review as a portfolio decision which business divisions are most useful in achieving long-run corporate-level goals.

Similar cycles are initiated and completed for other planning. Five-year plans and yearly budgets are examples. They differ from the cycle presented above in that the cycle consists of more steps, because functional managers within the division propose programs or estimate costs as part of divisional planning. Both top-down and bottom-up approaches to planning are encompassed in these planning cycles.

CONTINGENCY ASPECTS
OF FORMAL PLANNING

Although there are some common do's and don'ts of formal planning (Steiner and Schoolhammer, 1975), each planning system needs to be tailored to the particular organization and objectives it serves. It is evident that a corporate strategy and a business strategy are quite alike in a single product firm, and they are quite different in a multi-product enterprise where product/market planning is insufficient to establish corporate goals and strategy. A community college catering for two years to post-high school students has much less need for a complex multi-level planning process than does a multi-university that has three or more degree levels, a higher level of educated staff, a number of research institutes at many locations, and involvement in advanced-level education for many kinds of adults of all ages.

ENVIRONMENTAL PREDICTABILITY

It has been noted that under conditions of environmental stability, the internal need for organizational and task differentiation is less than that required when predictable variation in environmental factors occurs. Even less uncertain conditions may call for the development of alternate plans, one of which is to be evoked when it becomes clear which environmental situation the system is actually experiencing. The emergency room of a hospital classifies its potential workload and develops routines for each. This type of uncertainty is more predictable than a university uncertain of its legislative grants for operations. The latter must develop alternate proposals to follow, depending on what governmental action is ultimately taken, a unique, complex contingency planning task. Overall goals provide the point of departure for generating alternatives to meet contingent events.

ADAPTABILITY AND SLACK

Experience in a wide variety of tasks provides the skills required to better adapt to whatever situation comes to the attention of a unit. With flexible competencies, less detailed planning is needed to guide how potential changes should be handled. Similarly, if organizational slack is known to exist in an organization, wide variations in workload objectives can be accommodated and less precise planning can be tolerated. The health of a system is closely interrelated. If an engineering department has worked overtime for a number of weeks, plans to initiate a new product with its attendant heavy engineering workload might require delay. Good organizational health, breadth of experience, and slack allows lower precision levels in planning.

SIZE AND DIVERSITY

As organizations grow in size, more structural subunits develop. Planning, therefore, involves the involvement of more organizational units and a larger number of separate subgoals and plans than in a small organization, the planning for which may only be accomplished in the brain of its entrepreneurial president. As more organizational subunits plan, there also becomes a greater need to integrate the separate plans into the whole. Complexity of integration increases with size although not necessarily proportionately.

Complexity of planning is also introduced as the nature of operations in subunits becomes more diverse. Planning for the individual units in a chain of 500 consumer credit offices may be much simpler than planning for a manufacturing company with only a dozen different businesses. The lack of great diversity for the units of the consumer finance group allows similar planning for each. Each of the twelve manufacturing businesses under a single corporate umbrella may require separate objectives, planning processes, and planning systems.

EXPERIENCE IN PLANNING

As the introduction to this chapter noted, the great rise in planning activity and concepts has developed in the last twenty years. Planning was not unknown before that time, but its sophistication and degree of use has advanced rapidly during the past two decades. As a result, many corporations are babes in the woods as far as formally integrated long-range planning is concerned. Those firms with mature systems have a workable set of systems well linked with each other and to overall goals. Neophytes to planning focus on short-run financial or profitability planning. These systems may start out as no more than multi-year projections of the budgeting processes that such firms may have done for some time. As such enterprises experience the suboptimization of long-run goals from the overemphasis of its managers upon short-run profits, they start to change toward a comprehensive strategic and long-range planning system.

PLANNING AND GOALS

At each level of planning and at each stage, there is either explicit or implicit attention to goals. The formal planning systems in sophisticated organizations encompass the goal establishment process along with the strategies, major programs, and operating plans undertaken. Thus, goals and their determination are a part of formal planning processes. In addition, one can consider that the formal planning system stems from goals to be achieved, and it is a major method that private and public enterprises employ to achieve their goals.

SUMMARY

This chapter has examined formal planning as a systematic and rational method of translating overall goals to internal systems and operating actions. Formal planning has two aims:

    A.   Adaptation of what the organization is doing to the external environment and its realities.

    B.   Integrating internal operations to link them in a rational fashion with overall objectives.

Formal planning is more successful in dealing with integration than it is with the adaptation purpose. As a consequence, a major focus of the chapter was to examine internal resource planning as systems designed and operated to systematically connect internal operations of business strategy and business goals.

It is clear that formal planning results in higher levels of achievement than informal planning or no planning. These results stem from the inability of large organizations to determine the effects of changes upon internal operations. The complexity of large-scale organizations requires a formalized means of gathering all relevant data to major decisions through formal planning. The dynamic variability of social, technological, and economic factors in the environment also require the analyses provided by formal planning to estimate their relevance to an organization.

The analysis in this chapter has taken goals and strategies down to the point that multiple objectives at the level of each manager in an organization are shown to be necessary. As a final linking mechanism, the next chapter examines MBO and other performance evaluation systems at the manager's level to show the final coupling between overall goals and managerial behavior.

6

Management by Objectives

There has been considerable attention to the development and use of Management by Objectives programs in recent years. The initial impetus to the concepts of MBO can be traced to the "manager's letter." Drucker (1954) suggested that each subordinate write a letter to his boss periodically to describe his boss' objectives, his role in helping achieve them, how he would be measured, and what standards of performance constituted acceptable levels of performance. The letter provided a basis of discussion between the superior and subordinate about what was expected of the latter and a basis for review of actual results. MBO has come a long way since that first suggestion. A 1977 conference on MBO listed over fifty different speakers. The manager's letter has grown into a fad, according to some. It has become the consultant's cash cow. MBO is hailed as more than mere performance evaluation. MBO is a "new system of managing" (Odiorne 1965). In spite of the publicity and faddish atmosphere that ultimately spelled the end of other "savior" systems (for example, zero defects), MBO may survive in some form, because it can form a sound basis for extending the planning process from the top down to the level of managerial behavior.

WHAT IS MBO?

1. MBO is a type of planning process between a superior and a subordinate to jointly establish closed-end objectives for the subordinate to achieve within a specific period, usually one year.

2. MBO is also a means for control of subordinate behavior, because closing the loop at the end of the period involves a joint review of the subordinate's actual performance together with judgments about how well that performance measured up to results originally expected at the start of the period.

3. MBO is sometimes referred to as a system, because it is used commonly throughout an organization. Standardized forms, review periods, due dates, and reports to some staff organization (such as the office of management development) are employed. Analyses of MBO factors that are useful organization-wide are prepared.

4. Whether or not the organization as a whole utilizes MBO, any manager can employ the same process with subordinates as a means of linking their achievements to goals of the larger organization.

ASSUMPTIONS IN MBO

For the purposes of this book, MBO represents another link between overall organizational objectives and the behavior of individual managers. It is the type and intensity of the actions that individuals undertake that determine the results that an organization achieves. Throughout, we have been concerned with goal setting and developing strategies to achieve them as means for channeling behavior in goal oriented directions. MBO does this in a more specific way because closed-end time constrained results are established. The goals of a business unit in a multi-product firm would constitute the basis for initial development of MBO goals for the general manager in charge of that unit. Thus, MBO is to be thought of as a parallel system directly related to other planning efforts in which the manager is involved. MBO goals need to be consistent and coupled directly with other formal planning and control efforts.

A second presumption of MBO systems is that MBO will direct subordinates in the proper directions to higher result levels. By clarifying and establishing achievable goals that are relevant to all the desired aims, the expected results of an MBO system can be met. Yet, there is a long series of steps in the MBO process that can, if done poorly, invalidate this proposition.

A third assumption is that improved results can come from a review and feedback process that compares actual to expected performance. This assumption is much more tenuous, since learning depends upon rapid feedback, not yearly reviews as is typical in the operation of MBO systems. More attention will be given to this assumption in the analysis to follow.

WHAT OBJECTIVES SHOULD BE SET

MBO is a performance evaluation system whose factors are the goals of the organizational unit over which the manager being evaluated presides. The objectives of higher-level managers are broad and comprehensive. The goals of each subordinate need to be narrower but contribute to the overall goals. To identify the goals to be sought, a particular subordinate may first be asked to write a personal version of the overall objectives of the boss. With this broader perspective in mind, the objectives developed by a subordinate for his own position will less likely be unrelated or contribute only obliquely to higher-level objectives.

If the head of a product division in a multi-product firm has established an overall profit goal in terms of a return on investment objective, this overall goal translates into specific revenue or cost goals for each of his immediate subordinates. The marketing manager for the division, for example, will be expected to establish objectives so that the planned sales will contribute a specified amount of gross margin. To achieve the contribution specified, the marketing manager may well develop specific goals within his responsibility:

   —advertising and promotion budget
   —new product/market testing and introduction budget
   —goals about the relative mix of products that need to be
     sold to accomplish the contribution goal
   —volume and market share objectives needed to achieve
     planned contribution goals.

These goals stem primarily from the requirement by the general manager to achieve a return on investment goal. The marketing manager takes or is assigned a contributed margin goal and breaks that down into the subgoals that his group needs to achieve. Note that these same six goals of the marketing manager are all necessary for the advertising director to establish his own goals. The advertising budget represents a constraint on his expenditures. The volume, product mix, and new product goals are informative to the advertising director for what he is expected to achieve with the budget he has. How to achieve these desired results for the marketing manager constitutes the task of establishing the advertising director's goals.

RECURRING GOALS

Some objectives are ever recurring. They are rooted in the ordinary duties of the manager involved. One class of recurring duties is predictable as they stem from a continuous or periodic task assigned to the position. The sales manager plans territories, schedules, regional visits, and so on, as routine activities. The production manager buys raw materials and continuously transforms them into finished products. The dean of engineering schedules a relatively stable array of undergraduate courses in a semester. A production manager of auto assembly may have a goal to achieve:

1. an average 500 car per scheduled day rate of output within a 5 percent variance.

2. a quality level so that dealer allowances for field repairs average no more than $25.00 per car and do not exceed $175.-00 for any car.

3. an average cost per standard car of $3,255.

The production rate goal presumes that no less than 475 cars per day will be produced on any day the plant operates. Less than 475 cars on any day constitutes unfavorable performance. An average of 500 is expected. The measure of the goal of output has, then, both a target and an acceptable variance. But the variance has an absolute level beyond which the manager is not expected to deviate. The measure establishes acceptable and unsatisfactory performance levels. The quality goal is of the same character, but the cost goal is stated merely as a target level. All are stated in the form of closed-end objectives.

For recurring goals of a continuous or known periodic nature, both the predictability of activities and, therefore, the ease of establishing goals can become relatively routine. Another class of activities frequently occurs but is not regular. The manager of an automobile assembly plant may be expected to entertain visiting auto dealers and zone sales managers as they take plant visits. When they will arrive and how many there will be cannot be established at the time the goals are set. The major duties of some managers may not be periodic, but their statistical frequency and level often can be estimated. Disruption of the routine through telephone calls, conferences called, and meetings held is typical for the executive rather than exceptional.

Mintzberg (1973) found the following distribution of work of top executives:

	Hours	Number of Activities	Average Time
Desk work	22%	33%	15 minutes
Tours	3%	5%	11 minutes
Unscheduled meetings	10%	19%	12 minutes
Scheduled meetings	59%	19%	68 minutes
Telephone calls	6%	24%	6 minutes

Except for scheduled meetings, the brevity and interruptions of activity is perhaps the most revealing aspect of Mintzberg's results. Although desk work and scheduled meetings probably dealt with recurring activities and exceptions to them, the fragmented nature of executive work is most surprising. The idealized image of an executive sitting at his desk with his computer terminal making decisions and giving orders is just not accurate. He appears more a man of action than a man of thought.

The implications to goal setting are several. The manner in which the executive carries out his tasks is not necessarily relevant to his goal setting. What counts is what he is able to accomplish. Whether he accomplishes his goals by telephone or scheduled meetings is irrelevant. This is not to imply that the ends justify the means. As long as an executive's behavior is within societal limits, the manner of goal achievement, if effective, is a matter of personal style of the manager.

Nonetheless, the random nature of the events to which the manager must give attention places goal setting for such activities in a somewhat different light. Salesmen selling specialized equipment need to know the delivery dates that can be promised to customers. Since these dates depend upon the workload already scheduled, the production control department in the plant is likely to best understand and be able to figure out when delivery could reasonably be made. If the production control department takes a long time to respond to delivery requests, the likelihood that the customer will buy from a competitor increases. Fixing delivery dates is a competitive tool for the salesman. It is reasonable to set goals for response for delivery dates, such as "realistic delivery schedules will be provided forty-eight hours after receipt for 99 percent of requests received and in no case will response exceed seventy-two hours."

The production control manager does not know when or how many requests will be received. Nonetheless, this activity recurs. The workload is not continuous, periodic, or predictable for any day or week. The goal implies that, as requests vary, the intensity of delivery estimation work in the department changes. The task of the manager is to shift personnel to estimating delivery dates as that workload requires. To achieve his goal, the predictable recurring work may have to take a back seat priority until the unpredictable is within control. Of course, these kinds of balancing decisions are expected of responsible managers.

To provide complete information for the salesman selling specialized equipment, a number of other internal departments may also be involved. Goals for response to sales department requests need to be set for these other groups in conjunction with the response time objective of production control. For example, if a pricing group is estimating costs and margins for salesman's orders and has established a four-day goal of providing a firm price, it makes no sense to require production control to establish a forty-eight-hour deadline. Consistency among the several response goals appears more reasonable. The salesman cannot make a firm offer of sale until price, delivery, and, perhaps, other order specifications are received.

DEVELOPMENTAL GOALS

Establishing goals for recurring activities takes care of the already existing duties of a manager. The purpose is to ensure that the routine assignments are done well. There is nothing very sophisticated or creative about the activities or the goal setting process. Past experience guides MBO cycles for recurring events. Most good managers are not, however, satisfied with the status quo. What they seek are higher levels of performance and behavior. Thus, the director of data processing may plan to replace an existing computer with another. Automation of production scheduling, development of a new sales territory, bringing a radical new product on line, reorganization of a department, and similar plans constitute activities that are nonrecurring. They are designated as *developmental* for our purposes.

The risks of failure are greater for developmental goals than for recurring goals. In the subsequent evaluations of performance, consequently, the superior may be more lenient in his judgments about developmental results than he would be for routine goals. Over a longer period, of course, consistent success or failure to meet developmental goals is instructive as to the quality of formulation or implementation skills of the manager.   One executive was consistently coming up with innovative insightful approaches to improving his operations and those of his boss.   Yet, in most cases, the followthrough was weak.   Potentials were not realized, even though the risks were relatively high compared with operating-as-usual objectives.   The boss realized that, ideally, a manager should be able to achieve both creation and implementation goals.   Yet, he didn't want to lose the creativeness of the manager involved.   Consequently, he established a new staff position in which the man's creativeness could be expanded. He took the implementation out of the man's responsibility for followthrough by others.

Adapting a known technology for development is less risky and less creative than undertaking something that hasn't been done before. Today, it is possible to take off-the-shelf equipment and programs to automate labor cost and schedule data in unit production assembly operations.   When those systems were first visualized as a means of reducing large clerical costs, however, neither the concepts, the peripheral equipment to record plant activities, the computer technology, nor any experience by others existed.   A number of individuals spent ten to fifteen years of their lives developing and installing ever advanced versions of such systems, until today several available low cost systems can be used.   The risks of failures to the manager were relatively high during early development.   Today, they are not routine, but the risks are considerably lower.   The creativeness, failures, and searching of early developers are accommodated in existing available systems.

PERSONAL GOALS

While every manager will, under an MBO system, establish a number of objectives for his recurring responsibilities and may undertake developmental activities on a more or less constant basis, it is less probable that most managers will spend a large proportion of their time working toward personal development goals.   Executives new to the organization or individuals occupying a position new to them will, of course, attend to learning about the new tasks and environment. Perhaps the major portion of trainee time will be directed toward personal development.

The means for accomplishing personal development fall into three categories.   First are the part-time assignments, whose objective is to provide a needed breadth or skill in carrying out present or proposed positions.   Secondly, a few assignments are made on a full-time basis with the purpose of development for new positions in mind. The third category is education.

Part-Time Assignments

For the typical executive or manager, the need to establish personal development goals will emerge from the review of his performance in achieving goals in past periods. A sales manager who had had difficulty in paying sufficient attention to cost objectives may be asked to become a member of the divisional budget committee that reviews revenue and cost plans for all departments. The presumption of the assignment is that the sales manager will—through committee experience—gain knowledge of the whys and wherefores of cost control to apply to his own operation. In fact, the personal goal probably should be stated as a learning objective as well as one of meaningful participation on the committee. Of course, the tasks of the committee are presumably useful to the management of the division other than the opportunity it might provide for personal development.

Another kind of personal development goal involves assignments outside the firm. Community work or task force positions for governmental commissions provide opportunity for interaction in the wider community, while attending to externally imposed goals or constraints of the organization. Taking part in the activities of professional associations, for example, can provide contacts and insights useful in managing a university, hospital, or business firm.

Full-Time Assignments

The chief executive of a major chemical firm regularly employs several personal assistants selected on the basis of their potential for eventual top-level responsibilities in the organization. Their assignments are temporary, usually lasting two to three years. Then, they are reassigned to positions from which it is reasoned that the perspective achieved from association and assignments performed at top levels will be of benefit. As another example, some firms periodically and regularly rotate managers through a series of positions with the purpose of giving insight into the far-flung operations of the firm. While some job rotation is based upon such a need as determined from MBO evaluations, other rotation programs have developed from the generalized experience that the breadth of perceptions acquired provides upward mobility to the participants.

Both full-time and part-time work assignments for development should be meaningful tasks for the organization. The positions should not just be made up to meet personal development goals of one or more individuals. In positions that are merely make-work, responsible high potential managers are frustrated. They are not developed.

Formal Education

Educational goals are the third category of personal development activities. Executive and continuing education programs and courses of all types abound. Regular college courses are available. Some focus upon a particular new or complex system such as PERT/Cost or MBO. Organizations planning to adopt such systems utilize educational programs as one means of boning up on new techniques and approaches. Other programs are designed to broaden the conceptions and viewpoints of participants. Short courses such as "Financial Management for the Nonfinancial Executive" are common. Longer programs are designed to broaden the viewpoint of executives from that of a particular functional specialty to the complex multi-functional general management tasks.

In the establishment of personal goals, the closed-end objective ought to be stated in terms of the results that are expected of the subordinate rather than the activity. Further, it should be well understood between the superior and subordinate why that result agreed upon is a good thing for the man and the organization. Personal goals need to be tied into what the individual is expected to achieve at some later time in the organization.

To put into operation the ideas in the previous paragraph, consider a production manager that has set hard objectives for his organization in the past, has achieved those objectives, and has developed an organization of people and other resources of high quality such that foreseeable future requirements have been taken care of. Remaining as production manager in an already well-oiled and effectively operating group may offer little challenge to the manager, particularly if a capable replacement has been trained to manage in the production manager's absence. Under such conditions, it may be useful to the organization if personal goals are established for him to broaden his managerial outlook beyond production, with the goal in mind that as positions at the level of general manager opened up in the organization, the production manager would become a candidate for the opening.

A personal goal at that point in time could reasonably be established as: "to acquire the broad multi-functional and environmental perspectives, knowledge, and skills necessary to lead and manage an organization at a general management level. In particular, the learning ought to include an understanding of establishing goals for an autonomous business unit, dealing with strategic issues for a whole business, and dealing with subordinates in functions with which no direct previous experience has been gained. This learning is to be accomplished in one year."

Note that the personal objective does not interfere with recurring or developmental objectives of the manager, since these have been well taken care of in the past. The personal objective meets the needs of the individual and the organization and is stated in learning terms rather than as "to take a general management executive program." How to achieve the objective can constitute a learning experience itself. The production manager's superior is, in all likelihood, a general manager himself, so that he could assign the manager as his assistant general manager. There may be other internal alternatives of this nature, but an educational program designed to meet the needs of potential general managers may be the alternative thought to be best. The range of alternatives here is large, so reference to staff experts about the problem is warranted. Consultation with the director of management development about how and where any education to meet the goal could be undertaken would appear to be in order.

Education has become so popular in some arenas that it approaches the popular norm of behavior or even faddishness, rather than a means for achieving a personal development goal on the part of the manager. The writer was surprised to see in the audience of an executive seminar a governmental manager who attended a previous session of the same program. Asked why he was there, the manager replied, "It is my turn to attend." If educational attendance is thought of as a right, a reward, or an intellectual vacation, it is improbable that the experience will be of value to anyone. Unless personal developmental goals are being sought, the time and expense of attendance are less likely to be of organizational benefit. Although general education is a valuable asset to society, managers question whether their organizations are the vehicles through which this background is to be attained.

GOAL LEVELS

Chapters one and three addressed issues relating to goal levels, so intensive coverage of them is not repeated here. In an MBO context, the following summary and extension is offered.

1. Hard goals generate higher achievement than easy ones.
2. Extremely difficult goals are frustrating, in that they appear impossible to achieve.
3. Organizational learning suggests that one period's goal levels should exceed the prior period's.
4. Goal levels tend to settle somewhat higher than past performance. As performance improves, goal levels advance. As performance declines, aspiration level goals also decline.

These are general suggestions that could be summarized as: "Set challenging but achievable objectives." When establishing MBO goal levels, however, the specific circumstances surrounding the subordinate's organization should be considered. If more efficient equipment is being installed, the production manager should anticipate improvement in the cost per unit goal. If a project to introduce an existing product into a new region is not to be completed during the interval covered by the goal setting process, an intermediate level of achievement can be established. If the product is expected ultimately to take 25 percent of the market share in the region, for example, what degree of that penetration will be achieved at the end of the evaluation period?

Past rates of change and their causes can be analyzed for insightfulness in establishing the levels for objectives. A thorough job in such analysis may require substantial data and analysis of it in preparation for the superior-subordinate goal setting meeting. The president of a firm kept seeking the same rapid sales growth that had been experienced in past periods from his marketing vice-president. At one meeting, the vice-president brought out the vulnerability of the firm to antitrust action because of the firm's market dominance in certain product lines. He questioned further growth in those lines, suggesting that future sales growth should come primarily from new products rather than greater market penetration with present products. He had tentatively developed his own view of his set of goals by emphasizing the sale of the most profitable products in the existing line. His goal was to increase profit contributions at rates as great as in the past, but the increased profits would come from product mix changes rather than from increased sales volume. This example shows the specific kinds of analysis necessary to match a manager's goals realistically to other plans.

SPECIFIC GOALS

An MBO system of planning and review depends upon objectives being stated in specific operationally measurable terms. An objective "to increase the learning of our students" is too vague and imprecise. How does one measure what is to be achieved? In corporations, profit goals often dominate the reviews and attention, because profit is regularly measured. It is an accepted concept. It is to the unmeasurable and the difficult to measure, however, that attention often needs to be directed.

To "improve morale in the general staff management area" is so imprecise that when reviews of performance are conducted, the superior would be at a loss to know whether progress had been made or not. Without measures of morale, how is it clear that improvement is a proper goal in the first place? Indicators of performance are necessary else the MBO process flounders. Does the number of grievances filed indicate the presence or absence of good morale? Or does an attitude survey need to be validated to measure it? Personnel turnover? Absenteeism? Combinations of the above?

It is difficult to establish the areas or *content* of goals. It is more difficult to set realistic *levels* for future achievement. Developing valid *measures*, ones that truly indicate the status of a phenomenon, is just as difficult. Because establishing valid goals is not an easy task, it can be often slighted. So far as the MBO system has been established as an integral part of the planning and control systems of an organization, such failures jeopardize overall achievement.

GOAL SETTING
AND REVIEW PROCESS

In previous paragraphs, some insights have been given to the processes of MBO. To avoid repetition, detailed exposition is presented only when new ideas are relevant. The MBO process can be considered as a cycle of a number of stages carried out by a superior and a subordinate.

1. Prepare for goal setting meeting
   a. Subordinate
      —Describes the objectives of his superior.

       —Determines content of his goals: recurring

                             developmental

                             personal

       —Determines measures of goals and levels to be sought.

       —Develops a set of action plans to accomplish goals.

       —Prepares his statement for the superior.

   b. Superior

       —Develops goals he wants subordinate to accomplish during the period being planned.

2. Hold joint goal setting meeting. The purpose is to gain agreement upon expected performance of the subordinate during the next evaluation interval. What help is expected or needed is agreed upon as well as achievement. A signed, written agreement seals the commitment of both. Levels of satisfactory performance are preestablished and documented.

3. Hold evaluation meeting of results achieved. Using the goals set, an objective review of past performance relative to objectives agreed upon the joint goal setting meeting. The evaluation meeting has two purposes. First, how well did the individual manager perform? Were there unanticipated or uncontrollable events that changed what should have been achieved? If not, what was actually attained for each previously set goal? Overall, is this good or poor? Since the subordinate often has substantial backup data about the period's performance, decisions about how well the subordinate has done should await completion of the review meeting. The second purpose of the meeting is to counsel the subordinate about how performance could be enhanced.

The evaluation meeting occurs close to the end of the period during which the objectives previously established in the goal setting meeting were to be achieved. After a superior and subordinate have reviewed past performance to determine whether the subordinate has performed well or not, how can the meeting's results be used? Merely saying that an individual did poorly (or well) is not enough.

This chapter considers MBO as a parallel approach to planning, operating in conjunction with formal planning, strategy development, and organizational goal setting. MBO focuses on the goals of the manager; other systems focus on organizational goals and plans. Obviously, the two are related as the manager acts for the organization. MBO is also used in other contexts. Just as frequently as MBO is employed as a planning device, it is used as a means for managerial performance planning and review. There are many types of systems for performance evaluation, and MBO can service the same goals as most of them. The following uses of the results of MBO are couched in terms of what any type of performance planning and review system can attain.

ROLES OF PERFORMANCE EVALUATION

There are four primary roles served by formal systems of performance evaluation. Each of these is examined in this section. Performance evaluation consists of a formal review of the subordinate by his superior or others. Peer reviews in hospitals evaluate the individual doctor's diagnosis, tests ordered, and treatment. Performance evaluation by faculty peers in a university often are associated with decisions for granting permanent tenure and promotions in professorial rank. Although variations exist in who reviews whom, in formal organizations, most performance planning and evaluation centers upon the superior-subordinate relation. It should be noted that considerable emphasis in some systems is placed upon self-evaluation, a bottom-up rather than a top-down approach.

Performance planning can be undertaken to set forth what is to be accomplished in the future, both from the point of view of the job and what the individual might undertake to do in a personal way to improve his job performance. If a subordinate's lackadaisical attitude is getting a poor reception from others, setting plans to attempt to change the attitude might well be in order. In a coordinated system for performance planning and evaluation, both job and personal plans are established, and then later, performance toward these plans is reviewed and evaluated. Most such systems are simply called performance evaluation or performance reviews, even though the total system also includes planning the expected performance levels for future periods.

IMPROVEMENT IN PRESENT POSITION

A major objective—perhaps *the* major objective—of performance evaluation systems is to improve job performance by the individual in tasks of the current position in the organization. All organizations exhibit learning such that the overall performance improves over time (Cyert and March 1963). To maintain a competitive position, each enterprise must learn at rates equal or better than competitors. Although there is performance improvement stemming from mere repetition of decisions and tasks, the rate of improvement can be accelerated if improvement and development efforts are focused upon minimizing weaknesses and emphasizing strengths.

The manager of a large communications group was in charge of worldwide interplant telephone, computer, and telecommunication systems together with the printing and reproduction of voluminous reports. The manager was highly innovative, constantly introducing new and evolving techniques and systems. At the same time, the costs per message and the costs per printed page were erratic and increasing. In a yearly review of personal job performance, it was noted that her subordinate managers and operating personnel never had the time to get acquainted with one system before it was changed or replaced, such that potentially beneficial learning curve effects did not accumulate. The group required systemizing and stabilization to achieve cost reductions. While innovations in processes had been useful, their rates of introduction had been excessive. Upon recognizing this, the manager turned to establishing certainty and a more moderate level of change. Her change in behavior resulted in significant performance improvements. This behavior change was not brought about by altering her attitudes, knowledge, skill, or education. Behavior changed and improvement resulted; channeling activity generated the improvement.

DEVELOPMENT

Although the previous example focused upon redirecting behavior to improve current performance levels, increasing the output of managers frequently involves their reeducation. When individuals in technical positions of a nonmanagerial nature are first promoted into supervisional and managerial ranks, for example, they often have no prior education of how to manage. Handling a set of accounting books properly involves technical knowledge that might include economics, taxes, insurance, accounting, overhead allocation, pricing, and so forth. If the person handling this task were to be promoted to supervise other accountants, taking care of their personal needs on the job, their motivation, their development, their pay, and interpreting company policy to accounting personnel are examples of the new work content involved. Mere observation, osmosis, and even experience in management rarely is adequate to provide executive knowledge and skills. Development to shore up weak spots and to use the individual's strengths to best advantage in the managerial task constitute enlightened developmental effort.

The developmental needs are uncovered through some sort of performance evaluation system that identifies the manager's strengths and weaknesses, where developmental effort is most critical, and perhaps, how the manager in question can best apply efforts to become better prepared. Of course, development is a type of learning. Teachers do not make anyone learn anything; individuals learn. The teacher provides learning opportunities. Thus, management development is said to be self-development. Although his superior may get a sales manager appointed to a new products committee to broaden his viewpoints about the goals and constraints the firm faces in product innovation, the sales manager can subvert this developmental intent if he merely attends and ignores the content and processes of the committee as they may be useful in better understanding his job. In addition to providing opportunity, motivation toward improvement also is critical. For development purposes, the evaluation process usually focuses upon developing characteristics that are needed on the individual's present job rather than what the individual might need to do to prepare for advanced executive levels. The first requirement for promotion is above-average performance in one's present position.

LEARNING

The improvement and development purposes of performance evaluation are forms of learning. One learns to do a better job on the current assignment or learns skills useful in a broader context of the organization. Learning theory instructs us that the sooner feedback occurs after the behavior is observed, the more likely it is that the individual will learn from the experience. In the classroom, exams that are returned at the class period immediately after the one in which the exam was taken are more effective in correcting misconceptions about the subject than ones returned a month later. Feedback while the topic is fresh in the learner's mind improves both motivation and knowledge.

In light of learning theory, managers cannot rely upon performance evaluation systems alone to meet improvement and developmental goals. Rather, more frequent timely feedback to critique performance is called for. One type of evaluation identifies only the unusually good or bad incidents of behavior to use in periodic discussions with subordinates. The *critical incident* method of evaluation is the result. As the incidents occur, the superior counsels the subordinate. Yearly or six-month reviews are then *cumulative* judgments about behavior. They do not focus only on recent events, and they are not relied on exclusively for learning.

PROMOTION AND MANPOWER PLANNING

The results of performance evaluation systems can be designed to provide data useful in managerial manpower planning and the implementation of such plans through reassignment and promotion of managers. If a system indicates the readiness of an individual to undertake increased responsibilities, direct upward movement in his chain of command is an obvious possibility. Thus, the performance evaluation of the subordinates of a retiring manager provides, at least, information as to whether any of them could be considered candidates for the vacated position. When positions open up in departments somewhat removed from the one in which a potential "comer" is located, some means of matching the open managerial position to the potentially qualified manager is needed. In some organizations, a data file identifying high potential managers is kept. When a managerial opening occurs, matching the job requirements to the coded qualifications of individuals in the reservoir generates a list of potential candidates. The data bank on high potential individuals can make past performance evaluations available. More importantly, individuals in the high potential group would not be there if performance evaluations did not show superior levels of past achievement as well as potential for higher levels of responsibility.

SALARY ADMINISTRATION

A final major purpose of performance evaluation systems is to provide the rationale for managerial compensation. The equity among individuals of periodic wage adjustments is frequently based upon judgments concerning an individual's past contributions and future potential. Without a systematic unbiased method of evaluating them, managers will perceive the system as unfair. Criticisms, appeals, resignations, and lowered incentives can stem from unsystematic approaches. Yet, performance evaluations must be individualized to reflect the personal contributions of the manager being evaluated.

Managerial compensation systems frequently possess both a basic portion that establishes minimum salary for a period and an incentive portion. The proportion of variable compensation depends, in sophisticated systems, upon the extent to which the manager achieves the goals of the business unit of which he is a part. If the business is a cash cow, increases in market share and overall volume are *not* reasonable goals to achieve; maximizing cash returns and maintaining market share could be expected. During the same time period, expectations concerning goals to reduce pollution and to provide certain levels of managerial development may also have been established. Performance evaluation provides a means for the superior to make judgments concerning how well the subordinate has achieved those duties previously established and, as a result, the amount of variable compensation the individual is to receive.

CONFLICTING OBJECTIVES
OF PERFORMANCE EVALUATION

Attempts to design integrated performance evaluation systems soon face up to the conflict between (1) salary administration and (2) both the improvement and development goals. Salary administration, especially determining and communicating results to subordinates, is evaluative, sometimes critical, and often ego deflating. The atmosphere in judgmental meetings between superior and subordinate to arrive at the subordinate's bonus is not amicable to the counseling atmosphere that one wants to create in evaluation reviews for improvement or development. Obviously, there are close connections between performance achieved and the need (or lack thereof) for improvement and development. Yet most consultants and practitioners (Fournies 1974) caution that a meeting to address both goals simultaneously just does not work in practice. At the very least, superior-subordinate interviews for salary discussions should be separated from those related to counseling about development and better performance.

Similarly, the goals of evaluating past performance and future potential are conflicting objectives. If both purposes are attempted in a conference between superior and subordinate, the discussion tends to lose sight of the improvement needed in the current tasks confronting the two persons. It is more pleasant to contemplate what the future holds than to get down to basics about what's wrong now (Odiorne 1965).

MBO IN PERSPECTIVE

MBO is a system of performance evaluation to be sure, but it is somewhat more than that. Through the superior-subordinate meetings, a manager learns where he stands. Communication about what is expected and how well he is performing provides an explicit means of guiding subordinates to desire directions.

MBO provides the opportunity to tie in the goals of managers at each level to those at the next higher level. If carried out logically and ideally, the goals at each level would be contributing most directly toward overall organizational objectives. Suboptimization, goal displacement, and satisficing behaviors would tend to be minimized, as goal hierarchy matched organizational hierarchy and both are integrated with top-level goals.

A good MBO process is fair. Bias and distortion are minimized when attention is focused upon output rather than upon personal attributes or behavioral idiosyncrasies. More objective and valid measures of results are possible than with alternate approaches that rate attitudes, values, and actions of subordinates.

MBO provides a potential method of integrating the physical, financial, and human resource plans of the organization to the goals that an individual is expected to achieve.

Given all these potential benefits of MBO, one would expect widespread applause and enthusiastic endorsement for it. Yet MBO has not lived up to the expectations that many have had for it. Many systems just have not worked, and others have delivered reluctantly. Although some successes exist, it is surprising that more do not appear. Analysis of success and failure is instructive. This chapter concludes with summaries of research on the subject.

PITFALLS IN MANAGEMENT BY OBJECTIVES

COMMITMENT

As we have seen, MBO systems are difficult to operate well. Not only must each executive delve into a complex problem as he works out his goals with his superior, he also must do the same with each of his subordinate managers.

If MBO is not linked with other planning, some rationale for it is lost. Given the perceived high workload in implementing an acceptable program, any lack of rationale tends to destroy executive confidence and commitment to it.

Executive commitment to the value and operation of MBO is the most important factor involved in its success or failure.

DESIGN

Technical errors in the scheme or operation of an MBO system can have a deadly effect upon its functional success. Instructions to combine salary reviews with those for evaluation and improvement in current performance would cause major difficulty in operation.

FAILURES IN PREPARATION

If both subordinate and superior come to a goal setting meeting or a performance review meeting without substantial support and backup, the likelihood of the meeting achieving its ends is substantially reduced. Similarly, if counsel for improvement is to be relevant to the individual's job, considerable analysis may be required to arrive at an optimal plan for development.

FOCUS ON PERSONALITY

Skilled psychologists may have difficulty in identifying reasons behind an individual's behavior. For managers relatively unskilled in personality analysis, the difficulty is compounded. Even if one is skilled in analysis, the personality traits of good versus bad executives are not clearly established. Therefore, focus on personality analysis is not warranted in performance review sessions.

MBO systems, as described in this section, avoid dealing with personality, but they do deal with the person. In setting goals for personal development, the specific knowledge or skills needed for the person to better perform are addressed as personal goals. Personality, attitudes, and values are avoided; improved abilities are emphasized.

SUMMARY

It is perhaps trite to conclude that pitfalls in MBO systems stem from design, operational, or commitment shortcomings. The same might be said of an accounting or wage payment system. Commitment pitfalls are perhaps different for any optional system within an organization. Unless the need for a system is externally imposed by law or negotiation, commitment to it may become a problem. MBO, or any other voluntarily developed system for managing, is dependent upon management support from the top to the bottom until it has become institutionalized as part of normal operating practice.

PERFORMANCE EVALUATION IN REVIEW

The reason that performance evaluation and, especially, Management by Objective systems have been the subject of a chapter in a book on goals is the impetus that they can provide to goal establishment and evaluation in an organization. Setting top-level objectives and attempting to achieve them merely through establishing suborganizational structures with specified duties allows substantial leeway for error and failure. MBO systems and job-factor oriented performance evaluation systems (if they are not one and the same thing) provide a mechanism for translating overall objectives to the lowest managerial level.

7

Goals and the General Manager

This book has been concerned with the development of goals and goal structures throughout the management organization. This examination is relevant, because without the constant integration of internal operations and external events to the purposes of an organization, its activities can soon be fragmented to provide little value to society or to the members of the organization.

GOAL HIERARCHY

Organizations are formed to achieve a purpose. If this were not so, the organization would have no rationale for being. At formation, strategy as a means for achieving the organizational objective is also required, else the enterprise might be able to do any number of things to achieve the same goal. To accomplish any substantial task, a rational organization is required. From this is established an organizational and managerial hierarchy.

To ensure that suborganizations are integrated with the original objective of the organization and its strategy, goals for each of the suborganizations need to be developed to clarify how the suborganization is to contribute to the overall objective. Concurrently, in rationalizing the role of each suborganization, the need for suborganization strategy becomes evident.   Thus, hierarchies of organizations, managers, goals, and strategies are implicit in any organization of more than a few people.   In small organizations, the formulation of these hierarchies may not be done in a formal rational manner.   As the organization grows to a size that its activities cannot be intimately known from personal observation, the need for formalized means for aligning goals and strategies in a hierarchical sense increases.

MULTIPLE GOALS

The original goal of the organization is not enough to ensure proper direction of activity toward meeting it.   If a group of entrepreneurs seeking profit try to maximize it, attention to the managerial, financial, and physical resources needed to accomplish profit over a long period of time are slighted.   Thus, it becomes necessary to establish multiple objectives for the organization as a whole.   Proper attention to direct activity in the several key areas (such as proposed by Drucker 1954) helps ensure viability of the system over time.   This same need for multiple objectives extends to lower levels of organization.   The rational establishment of goals leads not only to the hierarchy of objectives, but also to multiple goals for each manager at each level of organization.

Not only do multiple objectives stem from the need to enmesh lower-level goals with the overall objectives of the organization, but they also stem from the interactions that a suborganization at one level has with other suborganizations at the same level.   Thus, marketing activity and what it attempts to achieve in the way of goals is constrained by production activities, and vice versa.   In general, goals and constraints need to be rationalized wherever substantial interaction occurs, whether horizontally or vertically.

The pattern of goals in an organization at this point could be represented as a pyramidal matrix with the top of the pyramid representing the multiple goals at the top of the organization and each row representing objectives at one level of organization.   Some objectives in a row interact with each other, but in either event, the objectives at any one level interact with goals at higher and lower levels.

PLANNING AND CONTROL SYSTEMS

It is at this point (or before) of a complex of goals, strategies, and subgoals that the structure of them needs to be aligned and integrated with overall objectives. How does top management ensure rationality and linkage to the whole enterprise? A series of key systems for planning and control need to be developed to help ensure subordinate attention to overall purposes. A financial budgeting system is incorporated so that financial uses and controls can be related to the goals and strategy of each budgeted unit. A long-range planning system is introduced to extend the period of analysis so that short-run events do not overshadow the longer-run achievement of goals. Strategic reviews are initiated to ensure proper alignment of means to ends. MBO systems link immediate objectives to the goals of the organization that the manager heads.

SYSTEMS INTEGRATION

Some of the planning and control systems tend to focus on the rational development of a series of plans that further one *single* goal of the whole organization. Thus, resource allocation systems tend to focus upon ensuring that physical resource goals are met. The management development system focuses on managerial resource goals. Budget systems focus on financial results. Because the multiple goals are interrelated, the planning and control systems associated with separate goals also need to be integrated with each other. The resource allocation system cannot, in a rationally integrated organization, establish a goal of increasing capacity, while the management development system is attempting to reduce the number of managers to accommodate decline. The goals attended to by the separate planning and control systems need to be aligned to overall objectives. The responsibility for this integration lies at the general management level interacting with directors of the systems and the managers of operating units who need to contribute to the goals of the several system directors.

SYSTEMS FOR
EXTERNAL ANALYSIS

Not only do the overall goals need to be aligned internally in a horizontal and vertical sense within the pyramid of goals, but also attention to social, political, economic, and technological pressures and change needs to be given. Organizational groups are formed to monitor, analyze the effect of, and recommend means for adapting to environmental influences. Economic forecasting, market research, legislative liaison, technological forecasting, and social monitoring are examples of organizational subunits devoted to aligning overall organizational goals to environmental influence. In a way similar to internally oriented systems, these externally oriented ones tend to focus on a particular goal of the overall system. They need to be integrated with each other and to internal systems. Again, the general management level is the only organizational level at which this interrelation of external and internal needs can rationally be accommodated.

POLITICIZED INFLUENCES

To this point, recognition has been given only to rational approaches to aligning operations and environment to overall goals. We have in prior chapters also seen the influence of individual power and coalition operations that can and do distract from achieving overall goals. As the controller develops a budgeting system, the system is able to influence how resources are employed. Thus, the personal or professional goals of the controller can be furthered by his design and operation of the budgeting system. A coalition of the controller and others who think along the same lines can subvert the achievement of overall objectives to results that the coalition deems important. How can this be prevented? The general manager needs enough counteracting power (particularly through the compensation system) to influence system and operating managers to work toward overall goals. The general manager also needs to retain control of the key management systems, if overall results are to be maximized.

For external influences, the general manager has less power to counteract anything that might be detrimental to the enterprise. A major technological change that threatens to displace an existing product line can only be adapted to in some fashion. Rational adaptation requires information. As a consequence, the organizational systems for technological forecasting, social monitoring, and so on, play the role of intelligence gathering and interpretation, so that adaptation choices can be made. Again, it is at the general management level that these choices need to be finalized if external effects are to be properly integrated with overall goals and subgoals.

GENERAL MANAGEMENT:
THE KEY ROLES

Throughout, we have shown that the general manager is instrumental in aligning goal and strategy hierarchies, in developing multiple goals and constraints, in authorizing planning and control systems to attend to goals, to integrating planning and controls with each other and with the results of operating units, and in dealing with external and internal coalitions.   Although staff advice, recommendations from the managers of each of the planning and control systems, and the feedback of results from operating units constitute information upon which adaptation of the goals of the enterprise can be made and suborganizations aligned, none of these managers can be expected to make these decisions.   It is only at the general management level that an integrating perspective among these influences can be expected.

Because of the key role of the general manager, the remainder of this chapter is devoted to, first, a description of types of general managers.   This may be old hat to some readers, who may skip this initial portion.   The second section examines the roles exercised by general managers as they set goals and align their systems to them.

TYPES OF GENERAL MANAGERS

A general manager is an executive with no single functional responsibilities.   That is, the GM is not concerned with *personal* stewardship over a functional task such as buying, selling, stockkeeping, manufacturing, finance, or engineering.   At the same time, the lowest level GM has managers in charge of those major functional responsibilities reporting directly to the GM position.   In this sense, the GM has multi-functional responsibilities.   In a small single product business, the president and chairman of the board may be the only general manager in the organization:

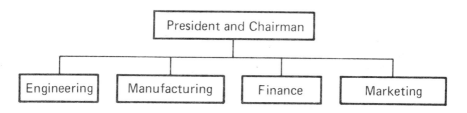

As the organization expands, there may be need for more full-time general managers in the system, so that the chairman and presidential positions are divided. Both are general managers.

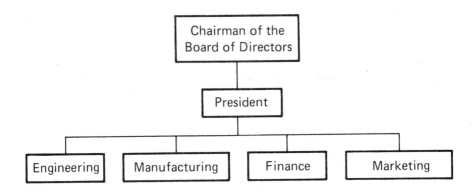

Further vertical task differentiation may occur by adding an executive vice-president as an additional general manager below the president. The proliferation of general managers occurs to a greater extent when the product line of the firm becomes so diversified that inefficiencies in coordinating the products or services through functional operations becomes burdensome or expensive. At that time, separate divisions, each to deal with the problems of a related line of products, provide the organizational forms to enhance coordination of the tasks of creating and distributing the products or services.

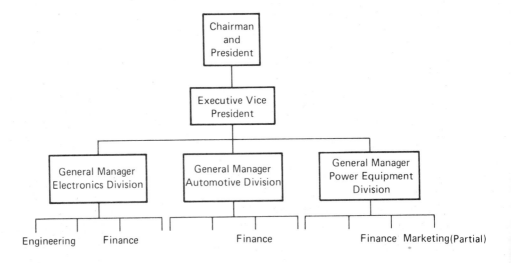

In the largest multi-product organizations, another level (or more) of general managers, often called "group" vice-presidents, may be added to the product division form of organization. It should be noted in the last chart that the executive vice-president is no longer supervising functional managers but is concerned with supervising a group of other general managers.

The proliferation of general managers in large-scale enterprises is not limited to business firms. At the top management levels of large universities, the chancellor-president or the president-provost dichotomy is common. This is similar to the president-chairman split. Further, each college dean provides a series of educational and research programs that are akin to separate product lines in a business firm. The dean of a college is in a general management position similar to that of a product line divisional manager in a profit seeking enterprise. Similar parallels could be sketched for governmental and other nonprofit systems.

GENERAL MANAGEMENT FUNCTIONS

To get at the relationship between the general manager's role and organizational goals, it is instructive to examine the roles that general managers must deal with, those functions that ordinarily would not be assigned exclusively to functional-level managers.

REPRESENTATION

As the leader of his organization, the general manager represents his organization to individuals and groups outside its legal or assigned boundaries. The chief executive represents the enterprise to stockbrokers, to alumni, to advisory boards, to shareholders, to governmental legislatures and officials, to major customers and suppliers, to consumer groups, and to social action groups. Without a clear conception of what goals the organization is to pursue combined with the strategies and subgoals contributing to overall directions, the chief executive is handicapped in representing the legitimacy and viability of the enterprise he leads.

Effective representation, then, involves articulation and justification of the organization's guiding philosophy, goals, master strategy, and objectives and strategies at the product/market level. Goals and constraints toward which the system allocates its energies both guide and stem from these strategic sources. Goals are developed, integrated, and communicated by the chief executive in light of the expectations that external individuals and groups have about the organization.

Lower-level general managers, for example, those at the business unit level of organization in a multi-product enterprise, fulfill a more limited representation role, although its nature is similar to that undertaken by the president. The general manager of a product division represents that business, its goals, strategies, and needs to higher levels of managers within the organization for justification of the legitimacy and viability of the product division within the total enterprise. Within the confines of the product division, the general manager has the internal-external bridging problems that the president has with the external environment. The division's plans, goals, and strategies cannot be developed in isolation from the larger organization of which it is a part. Rather, the division's subgoals need to enmesh with the master strategy of the firm. The growth rate objective of a division, for example, cannot exceed the capacity of the parent organization to supply the capital to fuel the growth. The division's environment is of two parts: the larger organization in which it resides and its relevant environments external to the corporate body.

Of course, representing an organization to its external constituencies is a task for any manager from foreman to president. The importance of external representation at the general manager's level assumes greater relevance than at functional or subfunctional levels, because it is at the general management level that potential autonomy of operation exists. A product division could, presumably, operate as a separate autonomous business; functional level organizations cannot. External coalitions and pressures are therefore more insistent at the general management level than at lower levels.

LEADERSHIP

The general manager is also the focal point for representation to individuals and groups within the organization. As a member of top management, the general manager is looked to by lower-level managers as representing the best source of overall direction. If the source of goals stem from an executive coalition of which the general manager is a member, the goals of the coalition for the organization need to be articulated to others, strategies shared, directions clarified. At the same time, the general manager needs to ensure that the key internal systems—resource allocation, planning, control, MBO, compensation, and so on,—are aligned in consonance with the goals and strategies at the general manager's level. The functional manager of plant and equipment in a business division cannot make rational plans unless the strategies for growth or decline that have been established for the division as a whole are known.

Leadership involves the establishment of strategy and goals together with getting subordinates to commit their energies to achieving the desired ends. Communicating ends and means for accomplishment becomes a central task of general managers as they develop and teach subordinates. All the sources of power, reward, coercive, expert, referent, and legitimate, are important to this leadership role.

In organizations dominated by other than an executive coalition, the general manager may not play an important role in formulation of goals. He may merely be the spokesman for the dominant coalition that establishes the purposes and directions of the enterprise. If the nonexecutive coalition is powerful enough to dominate goal choice, however, it ought to also be powerful enough to dictate the choice of the general manager. As a consequence, the general manager would in such instances constitute the leader and the representative of the dominant coalition.

STRATEGIZING

The general manager is intended to be the architect and builder of the goals and strategies the organization pursues. If the manager seeks to represent or to lead without goals and an accompanying strategy, then generalities, vagueness, and imprecision, if not vacillation, in communication results. Then, both leadership and representation suffer. While certain types of functional managers are critically central to the development and implementation of a particular strategy (for example, production and financial control executives for a defender strategy), it is only at the general management level that the balance in design and operation of the system can effectively be rationalized. Thus, the role of marketing or engineering in a defender strategy needs to be subsumed to that of production and control, if the strategy is to become most efficiently managed. The choice of balance to align functions and systems to overall goals cannot be delegated to submanagers. To do this would invite overemphasis upon subgoals in contradistinction to overall achievement. While suboptimization and displacement of top-level with lower-level goals can persist during periods of organizational slack, product or service maturities are inevitable. In competitive environments, slack ultimately will be eliminated.

In certain governmental enterprises, clouding the goals, strategies, and activities of the organization becomes the role of the general manager when the organization's task no longer provides the services originally intended. The bureaucracy in government is able to continue without being effectively reviewed as to effectiveness and efficiency, because the external competitive mechanisms are absent to force the need for review. Slack continues, subgoals of bureaucratic coalitions are maximized, and obsolete services are continued. The mayor of New York found, in financial emergencies, the extreme difficulty of identifying noncritical and inefficient services. Even when identified, strong political coalitions at times prevented rational action to be taken to eliminate them or to reduce their scope.

Under a rational arrangement, then, the general manager is in a position to formulate strategy. His success in rationalizing this process becomes the foundation for his representative and leadership roles. So far as the bureaucratic, expert, or politicized coalitions are able to obscure rational overall goals, the system and the general manager are forced to represent organizational activities to subgoal achievement, but in competitive, low slack conditions, the continuance of a system attending only to subgoals becomes questionable.

SUBOPTIMIZATION, GOAL DISPLACEMENT, AND ATTENTION TO SUBGOALS

The general manager is the only executive with the total responsibility for utilizing the resources of the organization in beneficial exchange with external constituencies. The general manager's need for balanced foresight is countered by the ambitions of subordinates to further their own suborganizational units. The general manager's considerable sources of power are thwarted by coalitions that challenge the ability of the general manager to integrate internal capabilities with external opportunities or threats. If subcoalition power is strong enough, the goals of the coalition displace overall goals. Suboptimization of overall goals occurs, but suboptimization can exist for other reasons as well (for example, a lack of clear communication of the general manager's goals). The relevance of this discussion to the general manager is that recognition of these processes as normal activities is necessary in order to counteract or to deal effectively with them. How can this be done?

SENSITIVITY

Recognizing when and where political activity is endangering the general manager's roles is critical if he is not to lose power. In a large organization, the general manager comes in contact with a limited number of persons. From them, inferences can be drawn as to which way the wind is blowing, but some managers go far beyond informal means of information gathering. Corporate staffs that investigate the affairs of functions within subordinate product divisions can be a source of information that discloses how well-coordinated subordinate activities are to corporate goals. Because the general manager has advanced through the managerial ranks, he has developed sensitivity to seek specific clues as to how subordinate organizations are operating. Whatever means are employed, a sensitivity to the felt needs of subordinates allows some recognition of suboptimizing activity and subgoal attention.

COOPTATION

Although the general manager may have considerable power to reassign individuals to isolated posts or to engage in similar tactics to minimize the effectiveness of a distracting coalition, a number of other tactics are available that are not viewed so unfavorably as is the blatant use of power. One such tactic is cooption, through which one attempts to get the potentially threatening individual or group to join him while still pursuing his own objectives.

The general manager of a product division had been assigned, in addition to the product line over which he had responsibility, an investment casting operation using the lost wax process. At that time, the lost wax process was in its industrial infancy, although the basic casting technology was known and used in antiquity. The new activity was partially a backward integration diversification since the cast parts could be used in products assembled by the division. The casting operation was losing money at substantial rates, so that overall profitability of the division was being pulled down. The division manager's immediate goal was to kill the project. He offered the investment castings manager a higher-level position in the division if he would recommend shutting down the casting operation. The cooptation tactic of the division manager didn't work, because the castings manager recognized that the higher-level management viewed his operation as a diversification move with hopefully high potential future sales. His formerly close association with corporate-level executives gave him additional power to resist the cooptation attempts by the product division manager. In spite of the failure in this example, cooption is a useful tactic in gaining additional internal power.

BARGAINING

Another tactic to employ to bring coalitions in line with general management goals is bargaining, whereby the general manager offers at first nonoperational, no-cost side payments to woo recalcitrant coalitions into line. If unsuccessful, substantive payments in terms of perquisites or effective policy changes may be required to accommodate the power and position of a particular coalition. Of course, threats and bluffing tactics (MacMillan 1978) constitute actions that might reasonably be attempted prior to trading away resources of importance to the overall system.

COOPERATION

If you can't beat 'em, join 'em. In some situations, the pervasiveness of the power of a subgroup overwhelms the system, and higher-level managers are able to survive only by cooperating with and joining the subgroup. While palace revolts are not frequent, they are good copy for the media and are, therefore, well publicized. A group of managers that had formerly been presidents of their corporations were dissatisfied with the operation of the conglomerate that had acquired their firms. The technical and managerial expertise of the former presidents was so vital to the continued successful operations of their businesses as part of the conglomerate that their dissatisfactions could not be ignored. Ultimately, the conglomerate decided to accommodate the dissatisfaction by selling the divisions headed by the dissident expresidents back to them on an earnings buyback arrangement. The future earnings of the divested firms formed the basis for repayment to the conglomerate. Although this cooperation was in the form of agreeing to disagree, the separations were amicable. Cooperation to meet the perceived needs of subordinates—even if such needs are at first thought to be inconsistent with general management's goals—may be preferable to continued discord.

SUBOPTIMIZATION AT THE
GENERAL MANAGEMENT LEVEL

The failure to maximize the achievement of a goal by any manager can result because of ignorance or uncertainty about information available to the decision maker as Chapter One has noted. Thus, the president of a single product functionally organized business firm may be facing such a turbulent customer demand environment that errors in establishing marketing strategies occur. As a result, goal maximizing fails to occur.

In multi-product firms, moreover, there is the demand from each of the product division general managers on corporate-level executives for resources to fuel growth or prevent decline in their particular organization. The task of corporate management is to determine the balance that should be achieved among the various product lines. The presidents of many universities have been faced with the dilemma of dealing with colleges of education and music education. Throughout much of the country, learning to play a musical instrument is a normal part of growing up. Many high school graduates want to transform the joys they experienced by playing in musical groups in their youth to a vocation. In fact, the desire is so popular that a widespread surplus of music educators exists. There are few jobs relative to the supply of candidates. When university resources are tight, presidents ask whether the expressed wishes of would-be teachers should be accommodated and, thus, maintain their musical education staffs to educate more teachers, or whether the realities of employment in musical education should be heeded to reduce faculty and staff in music education departments. The chairmen and deans of education contend that individuals have the right to a choice if education major students wish to enter. Yet, following that path of individual freedom to choose does not appear optimal from the point of view of the students, the university, or society at large in the long-run.

In multi-product or multi-service organizations, the corporate level officers thus have a portfolio of subenterprises to encourage, discourage, maintain, or divest. As new opportunities arise, a decision to enter a new line of activity to increase the diversity of offerings to its clientele is an additional possibility in the business portfolio choice. Some large builders and land developers have the flexibility to move from one product to another as demand shifts. Whereas during the 1960s, condominium resort development was profitable, the 1970s have brought precipitous declines in such developments.

Firms that have committed themselves to large investments in potential resort land tied up so much capital in them that they were unable to move into low-cost housing developments that began taking an increasing share of the available development market. Less committed firms retained the flexibility that allowed them to move much more rapidly.

The degree to which resources can be shifted to new strategic areas is an important constraint to the corporate business portfolio decision. For most organizations, the products and services cannot be shifted overnight. Strategic decisions to enter, leave, or to build a particular line of business take time. Although bending to the desires of peers, plans, and analyses of subordinate division managers for corporate support is an easy portfolio decision route, filling the pipelines with unneeded music educators also appears irresponsible. Sooner or later such suboptimization will reduce the slack available to develop those needed lines of future activity that the environment will support.

It is clear that suboptimization and overall goal displacement does not occur only within subsystems at functional levels and below. In multi-product firms, general managers, some with considerable power in important product lines, engage in self-seeking behaviors. Higher-level general managers must relate these sublevel pleas in a portfolio balancing sense to the master strategy and to overall corporate objectives.

THE KEY EXECUTIVE: THE GENERAL MANAGER

Although some strategies call for strong expertise in certain functions (for example, the prospector requires product development and marketing research executives), all strategies are dependent upon general management to ascertain the external-internal balance as well as to generate the leadership to efficiently provide the activities necessary to achieve the desired end objectives. The general manager is thus the keystone to the two sides of the arch of strategy: (1) environmental opportunities and threats versus (2) internal capabilities. Without the general manager's inputs, the structure would struggle to exist.

The legitimacy, effectiveness, and efficiency of organizational operations are dependent upon goals established and diligently pursued. The general manager provides the impetus to ensure that the environment, both internal and external, is served in balanced interests to both.

REFERENCES

Ackerman, R. W. "How Companies Respond to Social Demands." *Harvard Business Review* 51 (1973) : 88–98.

Ansoff, H. I.; Avner, J.; Brandenburg, R.; Portner, F. E.; and Radosevich, R. "Does Planning Pay? The Effect of Planning on Success of Acquisitions in American Firms." *Long Range Planning* 3 (1970): 2–7.

Armstrong, R. "The Passion that Rules Ralph Nader." *Fortune* 83 (1971) : 114.

Biggadike, R. "Entry, Strategy and Performance." Ph.D. dissertation, Harvard University, 1976.

Bower, J. L. *Managing the Resume Allocation Process.* Homewood, Ill.: Richard D. Irwin, 1972.

Bowman, E. H., and Haire, M. "A Strategic Posture Toward Corporate Social Responsibility." *California Management Review* 18 (1975): 49–58.

Burck, G. "The Hazards of Corporate Responsibility." *Fortune* 87 (1973) : 144.

Camillus, T. C. "Formal Planning: Creativity vs. Control." Ph.D. dissertation, Harvard Graduate School of Business Administration, Boston, 1973.

Carson, I. "The Big Leap in Corporate Planning." *International Management* 27 (1972): 25–28.

Chandler, A. *The Visible Hand.* Cambridge: Harvard University Press, 1977.

Christensen, C. R.; Berg, N. A.; and Salter, M. S. *Policy Formulation and Administration,* 7th ed. Homewood, Ill.: Richard D. Irwin, 1976.

Christensen, C. R.; Andrews, K. R.; and Bower, J. L. *Business Policy Text and Cases.* 3d ed. Homewood, Ill.: Richard D. Irwin, 1973.

Collins, O., and Moore, D. G. *The Organization Makers.* New York: Meredith Corp., 1970.

Cooper, A. C., and Schendel, D. "Strategic Responses to Technological Threats." *Business Horizons* 19 (1976): 61–69.

Cyert, R. M., and March, J. G. *A Behavioral Theory of the Firm.* Englewood Cliffs, N.J.: Prentice-Hall, 1963.

Davis, K. "Five Propositions for Social Responsibility." *Business Horizons* 18 (1975): 19–23.

Drucker, P. F. *The Practice of Management.* New York: Harper and Brothers, 1954.

Eilon, S. "Goals and Constraints." *Journal of Management Studies* 8 (1971): 292–303.

Fournies, F. F. "Why Management Appraisal Doesn't Help Develop Managers." *Management Review* 63 (1974): 19–24.

French, J. R. P., and Raven, B. "The Bases of Social Powers," in Dorwin Cartwright, ed. *Studies in Social Power.* Ann Arbor, Mich.: Institute for Social Research, 1959.

Friedman, M. "The Social Responsibility of Business is to Increase Profits." *New York Times Magazine* Sept. 13, 1970, 32.

Galbraith, J. and D. Nathanson. *Strategy Implementation: The Role of Structure and Process.* St. Paul: West Publishing Co., 1978.

Gibb, C. A. "Leadership," in G. Lindsey, ed. *Handbook of Social Psychology*, Vol. 2. Reading, Mass.: Addison-Wesley Publishing Co., 1954.

Granger, C. H. "The Heirarchy of Objectives," *Harvard Business Review* 42 (1964): 63–74.

Guth, W. D., and Tagiuri, R. "Personal Values and Corporate Strategies." *Harvard Business Review* 43 (1965): 122–132.

Hall, F. S. "Organization Goals: The Status of Theory and Research," in J. L. Livingstone, ed. *Managerial Accounting: The Behavioral Foundations.* Columbus, Ohio: Grid Inc., 1975.

Hatten, K., and Schendel, D. "Heterogeneity Within an Industry: Firm Conduct in the U.S. Brewing Industry 1952–1971." Working Paper 76–27, Harvard Graduate School of Business Administration, 1976.

Henderson, B. *Perspectives on Experience.* Boston, Mass.: The Boston Consulting Group, 1968.

Higginson, M. V. *Management Policies I.* New York: American Management Association, 1956.

Hofer, C., and Schendel, D. *Strategy Formulation: Analytical Concepts.* St. Paul: West Publishing Co., 1978.

Jacoby, N. H. "Capitalism and Contemporary Social Problems." *Sloan Management Review* 12 (1971): 33–43.

Karger, D. W., and Malik, Z. A. "Long Range Planning and Organizational Performance." *Long Range Planning* 8 (1975): 60–64.

Kotter, J. P. "Power, Dependence and Effective Management." *Harvard Business Review* 55 (1977): 125–136.

Krech, D. and Crutchfield, R. S. *Theory and Problems of Social Psychology.* New York: McGraw-Hill, 1948.

Lathum, G., and Yukel, G. "A Review of Research on the Application of Goal Setting in Organizations." *Academy of Management Journal* 18 (1975): 824–845.

Lawrence, P. R., and Lorsch, J. W. *Organization and Environment.* Homewood, Ill.: Richard D. Irwin, 1969.

Learned, E. P., and Sproat, A. T. *Organization Theory and Policy.* Homewood, Ill.: Richard D. Irwin, 1966.

Leavitt, T. "The Dangers of Social Responsibility." *Harvard Business Review* 37 (1958): 41–50.

Leavitt, T. "Marketing Myopia." *Harvard Business Review* 38 (1960): 45–56.

Lodge, G. C. "Business and the Changing Society." *Harvard Business Review* 52 (1974): 59–76.

Lorange, P. "Formal Planning Systems: Their Role in Strategy Formulation and Implementation," in *Business Policy and Planning Research: The State-of-the-Art Conference,* Pittsburgh, Pa.: 1977.

MacMillan, I. *Strategy Formulation: Political Concepts.* St. Paul: West Publishing Co., 1978.

Mace, M. L. *Directors: Myth and Reality.* Boston, Mass.: Division of Research, Harvard Graduate School of Business Administration, 1971.

March, J. G., and Simon, H. A. *Organizations.* New York: John Wiley & Sons, 1958.

McCaskey, M. B. "A Contingency Approach to Planning: Planning with Goals and Planning Without Goals." *Academy of Management Journal* 17 (1974): 281–291.

Mee, J. F. *Management Thought in a Dynamic Economy.* New York: New York University Press, 1963.

Miles, R., and Snow, C. *Organizational Strategy, Structure and Process.* New York: McGraw-Hill Book Co., Inc., 1978.

Mintzberg, H. *The Nature of Managerial Work.* New York: Harper & Row, Publishers, 1973.

Mintzberg, H. "Organizational Power and Goals," in *Policy and Planning Research Conference,* Pittsburgh, Pa. May, 1977.

Odiorne, G. S. *Management by Objectives.* New York: Pitman Publishing Corp., 1965.

Pitts, R. A. "Strategies and Structures for Diversification." *Academy of Management Journal* 20 (1977): 197–208.

Richards, M. D. "Providing Perspective to Management Theory," in Richards, ed. *Readings in Management,* 5th ed. Cincinnati, Oh.: South-Western Publishing Co., 1978.

Simon, H. A. "On the Concept of Organizational Goal." *Administrative Science Quarterly* 9 (1964): 1–22.

Simon, H. A. *The Sciences of the Artificial.* Cambridge, Mass.: The M.I.T. Press, 1969.

Sloan, A. P. *My Years with General Motors.* Garden City, N.Y.: Double-day and Co., 1964.

Steiner, G. A. and Schoolhammer, H. "Pitfalls in Multinational Long-Range Planning," *Long Range Planning* 8 (1975): 2–12.

Thompson, J. D. *Organizations In Action.* New York: McGraw-Hill Book Co., 1967.

Urwick, L. F. *Notes on the Theory of Organization.* New York: American Management Association, 1952.

Woodward, J. *Industrial Organization: Theory and Practice.* London: Oxford University Press, 1965.

Yankelovich, D. "Social Values," in The William Elliot Lectures, *Historical, Legal and Value Changes: Their Impact on Insurance,* University Park, Pa.: The College of Business Administration, The Pennsylvania State University, 1977.

Index

†